The Mobile DJ MBA

BUSINESS, SALES & MARKETING
Industry Secrets Revealed

A DJ Times Magazine Article Compilation

Stacy Zemon

*To Derek —
Wishing you great
success with
DJ Business!
— Stacy Zemon*

Dedication

This book is dedicated to disc jockeys everywhere
who work, play and live this profession.
Share your passion with the world
and recognize that true happiness
comes not from riches or praise
but from doing what you love.

Remember, great ability
reveals itself and develops
increasingly with effort.

You will know you are on the right path
when a series of naturally occurring
and meaningful "coincidences"
begin to happen as if
the Universe is conspiring to assist you.

- STACY ZEMON

Table of Contents

Acknowledgments

First, last, and always, I want to acknowledge and thank God, the source of life without whom neither this book nor I would have been written. Please continue to guide me in properly using the talents, intelligence and vision you have blessed me with, to be of service to others.

A BIG thank-you to the following people for their major contributions to this book: to Bobby Morganstein, for writing the inspiring and motivational foreword; to Bryan Durio, for meticulously proofreading my manuscript with a fine-tooth comb; to Mike Walter, for coming up with the title, "The Mobile DJ MBA"; to Robert Starkey, for his input and assistance with the cover design; and to Cap Capello for his advice regarding the Wedding Entertainment Agreement. Thanks also to everyone who sent me photographs for inclusion.

It is with sincere appreciation that I would also like to express my gratitude to the following individuals who have shared their best ideas and practices for the benefit of the readers of this book:

AL3, Mark Ashe, Rocky Bourg, Charlene Burg, Mitch Canter, Cap Capello, Steve Cie, Chris James DeGray, DJ Soulman, Brian Doyle, Mark Evans, Paul Evans, Scott "The Game Master" Faver, Lee Finkel, Betsy Fischer, Wes Flint, Bryan Foley, Aaron Foster, Tom "Fatman" French, Frank Garcia, David Gibson, David Hanscom, Mark Harmon, Steve Hoffman, Kevin Howard, Professor Jam, Jason Jani, Lisa Kasberg, Ron Keys, Kevin Kirouac, Kristin Korpos, Karl Langford, Sara Lavery, Brandon Lindsey, Mike LoBasso, Tom McCloskey, Ezra Mendoza, David "DJ Teddy Bear" Miller, Lisa Miller, John Mixon, Larry Neary, DJ Nexus, Kevin Nichols, Brian Nicks, Tom Ohlendorf, Stephanie & Jeff Padova, Marcello Pedalino, Matt Peterson, Lou Polino, Steve Rhodes, Rick "DJ Flip" Sajorta, J.R. Silva, Jamie Simpson, Gerry Siracusa, Robert Starkey, Mark

"Peace" Thomas, Adam Tiegs, Greg Tish, Randi "The Mitzvah Maven" Treibitz, Cheryl Quinlan, Sterling Valentine, Sid Vanderpool, Mike Walter, and Adam Weitz.

I also wish to acknowledge these fine companies for whom I am an Artist Representative: American DJ lighting, Promo Only CDs and DVDs, and GCI Technologies' Cortex HDC-1000 Digital Music Controller. Thank you Scott Davies, Brian Dowdle, Jim Robinson, Pete Werner, and Alan Cabasso for the opportunity to represent and use your fantastic sound, lighting, music and video products!

Last (but certainly not least), I wish to acknowledge you, the reader, for the investment you have made in this book. I am confident that you will gain valuable insight and prosper as a result of what you learn by reading it!

Introduction

What a great time it is to be a Mobile DJ Entertainer. Equipment technology and music delivery options are the best they have ever been and the number of skilled professionals in our industry is at an all-time high, thanks to the many educational resources and opportunities in the marketplace. What's more, social networking sites have opened up new forms of marketing to clients and communicating with other DJs from around the planet.

As I look out my window on this Friday morning I see snowflakes falling, which reminds me of how many long-time retail giants have fallen in the tough economy in which we live. When people have less money to spend on the non-necessities of life, it makes it hard for the small businessperson to stay afloat, let alone prosper under these conditions.

So what's a DJ to do? Well, it's a no-brainer that continuing to develop your talent and skills is a must, but here's the thing that so few in our profession really understand the importance of ... **EVEN IF YOU ARE THE BEST ENTERTAINER IN YOUR AREA, IF PEOPLE DON'T KNOW ABOUT YOU, THEY CAN'T HIRE YOU <u>AND</u> IF YOU CAN'T DEMONSTRATE YOUR VALUE, THEY WON'T PAY YOUR ASKING PRICE!**

The fact is that success is not determined by talent alone. Your "greatness" will not automatically attract new clients or trigger a flood of referrals. Other than talent, your long-term success lies in having excellent business practices, which includes the realm of marketing and sales. This is the key to financial rewards as a mobile DJ business owner. What you don't know <u>can</u> hurt you.

There are enough clients in your area who can afford your services and you can prosper despite general economic conditions – but only if you have the right tools and mindset. As a professional, I believe you actually have an obligation to market yourself effectively. In fact, you are doing your prospects a disservice by not letting them know about your services, and that's causing you to leave a lot of money on the table. You are here to share your gifts with the world but you can't do that if you can't be found.

When you run your business and conduct your sales and marketing efforts effectively, you will have the opportunity to attract more clients and make a greater contribution to people. The more you give, the more you get. The key to activating this powerful combination is to start giving.

Future clients are waiting for you to rock their party and give them an incredible story they can tell for the rest of their lives, so what are you waiting for? Dig into this book!

Yours faithfully,

Stacy Zemon

Foreword

By Bobby Morganstein

Owner: Bobby Morganstein Productions, Beat Street & Beat Street Station Party Rooms, Hour Entertainment, Enlight Lighting & Video
Producer: Complete Party CD Series & Complete "How To" Video Series
Winner: International DJ Expo "DJ of the Year" Competition (1999)
Inducted: American DJ Hall of Fame (2006)
Website: BobbyMorganstein.com

I've known Stacy Zemon for many years and was honored when she asked me to write the foreword to her latest book. I wasn't sure what to write at first but I think the best thing I can share with you is my history in our business.

I started out in 1981 working for a company called Fascinating Rhythm. Five years later I went solo as Bobby Morganstein, DJ Entertainer. In 1991 I expanded the company by adding three other DJs and we went by the name Frontline Productions. As a youth-oriented company that mainly did Bar/Bat Mitzvahs, I saw a need for good Jewish party music, so I produced The Complete Jewish Party CD. Shortly thereafter, The Latin Party CD and Novelty Party CD came along.

In 1992 I made my last company name change and incorporated as BMP Productions. I added more DJs, MCs and Party Dancers to the mix in our Huntingdon Valley, PA location. We used staging, backdrops, costumes, props and elaborate dance floor lighting to take Mitzvah entertainment to a whole new level in the area. The company was very successful and I thought that other mobile entertainment services from around the country could benefit from learning about what we do, so I produced The "How To" Bar/Bat Mitzvah Basic and Full Production videos.

In 1996 we expanded to six crews and opened the Beat Street Party Room. I also expanded our CD line to ten and our video line to five. A few years later we also expanded Beat Street to accommodate larger parties and in 2000, opened Beat Street Station. A couple of years later, we added Hour Entertainment, a company that offers clients novelty entertainment and photo favors for their cocktail hours. I opened a new company division in 2004 called Enlight, which provides intelligent lighting, plasmas and video screens not only for my entertainment company but for my local competitors as well.

In 2009, The Complete Party CD Series reached thirty-five CDs and expanded into digital distribution on iTunes. Twelve different DVDs are now available. We offer a full white setup in our productions and room-enhancing uplighting with customized gobos. We also introduced a lounge setup complete with sofas, funky chairs, ottomans and light-up tables.

Now that you've read my story, you're probably wondering what business, sales and marketing principles I used to build a multi-million dollar operation. Well, first and foremost I would say that I looked around for voids in the marketplace and filled them, meeting the needs/wants of clients and DJs alike. I wasn't afraid to take risks but they were always well-calculated and planned out. Owning a DJ business is fantastic but I always knew there was more I could add to upsell my clients, increase my bottom line, be a trend-setter and outdo my competition in the marketplace.

I am only one person, so it has been critical to surround myself with an excellent and dedicated staff to expand. Without them I would not own eight companies. I am proud of the fact that most of my employees have stayed with me for over ten years. I have always told them that one-third of the work happens before you ever get to the party, so make sure phone calls are returned quickly, that your client feels comfortable throughout the planning process, follow up after the event and stay in touch afterward.

No matter how many great ideas you may have for expansion, it's critical to add just one at a time and do it with the right splash. Showcase it, advertise it, add it for free to your parties and then let word-of-mouth advertising allow you to make money from your new venture!

I have always cared about doing the very best for my clients and therefore feel I have earned having a flawless reputation in my marketplace. I listen to what people want and offer suggestions if I think what they are asking for may not work. Ultimately though, the client has the last say and is always right. This philosophy has enabled me to build a reputation in which I have to spend very little on advertising and have primarily referral-based operations. All of my businesses are in a constant state of evolution. We continue to expand and make adjustments according to new changes in people's tastes. BMP stays adaptable and strives to be ahead of the curve, offering our clients cutting-edge technology and entertainment innovations.

Diversification is possible in the DJ industry. I am living proof of this fact. I don't think I will ever stop creating because there is a great "high" involved with having a new idea, researching it, making it a reality and then earning money from it.

In conclusion, I hope that after reading this Foreword and Stacy's book, you will be both inspired and motivated. Do you have a great idea for a new product, service, or division for your entertainment company? Then go ahead and take a risk. The marketplace is calling you!

Wishing you great success!

Bobby Morganstein

About The Author

Stacy Zemon has reached an audience of millions as a Radio, Club, Mobile and Karaoke DJ. Since 1979, she has entertained at over 2,000 private and corporate events nationwide.

Widely recognized as a distinguished industry leader, Stacy has made ground-breaking educational and business contributions. Since the mid-1990s, she has been writing business and feature articles for DJ Times magazine. Stacy is author of the world's best selling books for disc jockeys, *The Mobile DJ Handbook* and *The DJ Sales & Marketing Handbook*.

As an on-camera host for the Disc Jockey News Network, Stacy has provided live DJ trade show coverage since 2004. She has also been a keynote and featured speaker at DJ conventions, and is a regular judge at annual "DJ of the Year" competitions held at the International DJ Expo in Atlantic City, NJ.

Her roots began in radio, where Stacy has been an announcer, music director and program director in several formats. She pioneered a new business model between the radio and mobile DJ industries by forming a partnership with a national broadcasting company to operate as the mobile entertainment division for a chain of their radio stations.

Stacy is an Endorsed Artist of American DJ Lighting, Promo Only Music and Video, and GCI Technologies' Cortex Digital Music Controller.

She is committed to providing DJs with educational resources that support their long-term goals and help them to achieve prosperity.

AUTHOR'S NOTE: After reading *The Mobile DJ MBA*, I invite you to let me know how this book has helped you to grow and prosper at Stacy@ProMobileDJ.com. Also, if your company is in need of business, sales, marketing or copywriting services, please visit my business website at StacyZemon.com.

Developing Power Partnerships

As a DJ business owner, do you know the value of networking or the secrets to doing it well? At the heart of it, effective networking is about creating "power partnerships." Here are some tips to help you navigate these relationships.

A good place to begin is by joining your local Chamber of Commerce, Rotary Club, Lions Club, and Business Network International. Or you might try specialized business groups, religious organizations and fraternal societies. There are many local, regional and national DJ associations you can join.

How do you become a mingling maven? Remember, the best conversationalists do not merely ask a barrage of questions. They share stories, insights and ideas that are of interest to others. The big deal about small talk is that it is how we exchange information and opinions on issues. It's how we break the ice and get a sense of what people like and what they are like. It is the "schmoozing" that cements relationships.

When attending gatherings, most of the people with whom you come in contact will not personally be responsible for hiring the entertainment for their companies; however, they can find out who does and pass that information along to you. In addition, some of the people you do meet will be getting married, having birthday and anniversary parties, or even planning mitzvahs for their children.

A little creativity goes a long way toward creating opportunities to assist other members of any organization you join. Orlando, FL-based J.R. Silva sets a positive example. "I know a realtor who likes to call people who are selling their homes themselves. During the week, if I pass a house that has a 'For Sale by Owner' sign out front, I write down the phone number and address, and then deliver the lead to him at the next meeting. Don't you think this naturally makes him look for ways to help me and my business?"

Mark "Peace" Thomas of Awesome Entertainment in Los Angeles, CA, also believes that attitude is king when it comes to maximizing networking opportunities. "I've often heard business owners complain that 'their Chamber of Commerce does not work' or 'those DJ meetings are the same old tired stuff,' but networking is about making connections and all it takes is one person that believes in your service to turn those 'useless' meetings into gold."

Your USP

Just in case you haven't figured it out yet, you're not just a DJ. You're also a salesperson. Highly effective salespeople have a unique selling proposition (USP) that powerfully and succinctly conveys a compelling reason for someone to do business with you.

Developing a USP generally requires some soul-searching. Begin by contrasting and comparing your DJ Company with your competitors. Ask yourself, "What makes me and my services distinctive? What does my company offer that will be perceived by prospects as being of great value to them?"

Kevin Howard, president of Seattle-based The Howard Group and Sounds Unlimited, offers a persuasive reason to develop a USP for your DJ service. "It is important to remember that if you don't come up with a unique selling proposition, your prospects will; however, it may not be the one that you want. For example, a potential client may think you're unique because you're really expensive, whereas you would rather position yourself as providing the greatest value of any DJ service in your marketplace. People will always fill in the blanks when it comes to your sales presentation, so you need to be sure that you have clearly set forth your exceptional attributes in a crystal-clear manner."

You need to be able to verbalize your USP about who you are and what you do in a concise and understandable way. This is commonly known as your "elevator speech."

A great one succinctly and memorably introduces yourself and your business during a short elevator trip with someone (in about 30 seconds). Done well, it should "roll off your tongue" effortlessly, authentically and enthusiastically, and evoke interest in your DJ service. It can be used in formal business situations, on the supermarket checkout line, or while you're out getting your morning latte. To craft an impressive elevator speech, here are some steps to take:

1. Write down a brief explanation of your DJ services and your target market(s).

2. List the benefits that clients derive from hiring you as well as your competitive advantages.

3. Create an opening statement (hook) that will grab the listener's attention. It should be tantalizing, provocative and even funny or a bit mysterious.

4. Add a closing statement that is an open-ended question and will evoke a response other than "yes" or "no" from someone. It should be a question whose answer provides meaningful information to you.

5. Practice your finished elevator speech in front of a mirror. Record it and listen back. Do it in front of your significant other. Make it a contest for the best one among your employees. You will know you have succeeded in creating a good one when other people tell you so.

VIP Contacts

People do business with and refer business to people they know, like and trust. The key word is people, not companies.

Establishing a trusted network of very important people (VIPs) can be useful for a variety of purposes ranging from mutual referrals to strategic alliances. Your business life will run more smoothly and profitably if you create a network of loyal ambassadors comprised of key clients, referral sources and trusted advisors. Be sure to include staff members, friends, relatives and anyone in your "corner."

Today's flexible contact management and database software packages make it easy to catalog detailed information, code your lists and sort them by virtually any criteria imaginable.

Keep track of important personal dates, such as birthdays or anniversaries. Sending greeting cards on nontraditional holidays such as Thanksgiving or the Fourth of July instead of just the December holidays can make you stand apart from the masses.

If you read something that may be of interest to a "power partner," clip it out and send it along with a personal note. When you learn that a VIP has won an industry award or made it into the press, acknowledge the good news. In addition to sending a note of congratulations, you may want to ask the person's permission to mention the news in your company newsletter or on your website.

When a client or a colleague refers a prospect to you, always send a note of thanks. If a VIP mentions getting over a cold or leaving work early for a child's soccer game, follow up with a phone call in a day or so to check on the outcome. People are flattered when you inquire about their well-being.

Simply being thoughtful can build those all-important relationships that can make or break your business. Investing a few moments in communicating personally with key people can turn *contacts* into *contracts* – without a hard sell. If you continually benefit from someone and don't stay in contact or reciprocate back, you risk alienating him/her. Giving is good. "Paying it forward" is even better!

Complementary Businesses

A complementary business is one that offers products or services related to your business that may be of use to your clients. Chief among them are photographers, videographers, caterers, bridal stores, tuxedo shops, banquet facilities and limousine services.

You can propose "power partnerships" with complementary businesses that will help both parties reach potential customers at a lesser expense to either. Here are some ideas to assist you:

- Exchange links and banners on websites.

- Share advertising costs (e.g., print, direct mail, bridal fair exhibiting).

- Distribute marketing materials for each other at your places of business.

- Review each other's products or services on newsletters and websites.

Get to know the quality of a company's product or service as well as their professionalism and attitude toward customer service before making any kind of commitment. After all, it's your reputation on the line, so be cautious about who you recommend.

Referrals are a two-way street, and Lisa Miller of It's Your Party Entertainment in Phoenix, AZ, has the final word on the subject. "You don't ask someone to marry you on your first date, so why would you ask them to refer you immediately if you don't have a relationship with them? Don't expect to receive instant referrals if you're not willing to take the time and put forth the effort to get involved with people."

Selling Clients on Your Benefits

Here is a glimpse into the mind of the average prospect looking to hire a mobile DJ. "I need a DJ at my party who has lots of good songs so my guests will dance and have fun. I don't have very much left over in my budget. I wonder how much a DJ will cost?"

You and I know that as professional DJs we provide so much more than the typical person thinks about but before we can sell our services we must first educate potential clients. This is accomplished by effectively communicating the value of the multitude of services we offer.

Now repeat after me: "People buy benefits!" Human beings make purchases based on emotion, not logic. When logic and emotion come into conflict, emotion nearly always wins. Remember, people make emotional decisions and then create a logical argument to justify them. It's important to understand that your potential clients make buying choices because they want to solve a problem or fulfill a need. To be successful, you must deliver solutions.

The Flow of Selling

Features are the qualities or characteristics of your products, services or business. Benefits are the favorable results (value/solutions) that someone obtains from choosing your company.

To understand the benefits of the features you offer, think in terms of your prospect's needs and fears. To sell effectively, you need to be able to:

- Provide an answer to problems that people have or fear happening

- Represent the means of attaining their desires

- Inspire confidence in the quality of the solution

People perceive as offering a value greater than the cost. Bearing this in mind, the flow of your sales presentation should be to:

1. LISTEN to what your prospect wants and doesn't want

2. Describe the FEATURES of your company and their corresponding BENEFITS

3. Clearly explain how you can ensure that his/her EMOTIONAL NEEDS WILL BE FULFILLED

As you go through this process, be sure to use language the prospect has used and provide indications along the way that you REALLY listened well.

It's Time to Make a Very Important List

Here are some examples that clearly indicate the difference between a feature and a benefit. Try this for yourself, adding a third column for "Emotional Needs Fulfilled" (e.g., security, peace-of-mind, confidence, fun, romance, fear-reduction, acceptance, individuality and value).

Features	Client Benefits	E-Needs Fulfilled
Plasma Screens, Party Prop Packages, Party Motivators, Novelties and Musicians.	A more fun event for everyone attending. Greater guest interaction so they will stay longer. Enhancements help make client's occasion unique and memorable.	
Experienced DJ/MC Professionals with 10+ years of experience.	Experience and professionalism ensure that the music played will motivate client's guests to dance and have a good time.	

Features	Client Benefits	E-Needs Fulfilled
	Announcements will be made with polish and enthusiasm.	
Free event-planning services, unlimited consultations, online access to event agenda and music database, insured company, backup sound system on-site, written contract.	A fully customized event, a legitimate company, music coverage in case of an emergency and a written guarantee of services.	
A full-time business and member of a national professional DJ association.	A company that is highly professional in its operations and affiliations.	
Testimonials from former clients and other event professionals.	A company that has done a great job for others in the past and has a proven track record that the client can trust.	

The Ultimate Benefit to You

The more benefits you offer clients and emotional needs you can meet, the less important price becomes because now we are talking about VALUE. The greater your value, the higher price you can command.

Educated clients who understand the value of what you have to offer and who appreciate the results you deliver will become "referral-giving machines" and repeat customers. This, of course, means increased profits for your business and that's the ultimate benefit to you.

Going Ape over Guerrilla Marketing

DJ King Kong from New York felt like he was on top of the world as he realized his business had nearly doubled over the past two years. He beat his chest with pride, and gazed lovingly at his booking calendar. Kong knew this was no "happy accident." This was the result of his preparation, hard work, and persistence as a guerrilla marketer.

Perhaps you've heard of "guerrilla marketing" but don't know what it is. It is actually a loosely defined term that has been used as a descriptor for many types of non-traditional media such as viral marketing, grassroots marketing, and buzz marketing, to name a few.

This primer will assist you in understanding how, if you want to grow your business and be "DJ King Kong" in your market, you must remove the shackles of insecurity and fear and start going ape over guerrilla marketing.

Planning to Succeed

Guerrillas plan backwards, starting with a clear vision of the goal they want to achieve then creating a road map for attaining it. By knowing what must be accomplished and by when, you can shine a spotlight far ahead, illuminating the path upon which you are traveling and the destination to which it leads.

Put your vision into the form of a written plan and share it with your allies, which can include the VIPs in your life with a business background and marketing savvy.

To be highly effective, the plan for your marketing campaign must contain these key elements:

PROFITABILITY: Your advertising should bring in twice as much money as it costs to place (e.g., if you spend $100, you must net $300, or $200 profit). Track your advertising results in order to gauge how well each medium is working and to plan future expenditures.

CLIENT-FOCUSED: It focuses on your clients' needs and concerns rather than your attributes. Collect and use testimonials from former satisfied clients. Include a headline in your marketing materials that clearly states a benefit to the prospect.

SOLUTION-ORIENTED: It explains how your prospects' problems can be solved and their fears alleviated by engaging your services.

UNIQUENESS: It creatively and persuasively emphasizes what makes your services different and more desirable than your competitors'. If you don't already have a distinct USP (unique selling proposition) then create one. Effective advertising includes an irresistible offer your prospects can't refuse.

LONGEVITY: It motivates people to buy what you're offering and builds long-term value-based relationships.

Aaron Foster is a DJ, stage hypnotist and marketing expert. He believes all of these elements are important, but uniqueness comes in #1 in his book. "When you are unique, you can charge much more for your services. Think about it. Does your client want just a regular DJ company for their event or do they want outstanding, UNIQUE entertainment that will leave their guests wanting more and talking about for days, months and years?"

Achieving Maximum Results

There are several definitions for guerrilla marketing. This writer's personal favorite is: "Unconventional marketing intended to get maximum sales results from minimal resources."

Guerrilla marketers economize by getting the absolute most from any money they've invested in marketing. They realize that economizing has nothing to do with cost – and has everything to do with results.

Make the most out of your existing resources before spending your hard-earned dollars elsewhere. The best method of economizing is to market to your past clients. It costs a fraction as much to get a previously happy client to book you for another gig then it does to begin the courtship process with a new prospect.

Also, consider joining local organizations where you can build relationships that lead to referrals. Popular organizations include the Chamber of Commerce, Rotary Club, Lion's Club and Business Network International. There are ethnic and religious organizations, and fraternal societies, as well.

A solidly formed and well-executed marketing plan requires an investment. Stay patient and committed, and don't abandon your campaign before it has the chance to pay off. Guerrillas know that it takes time for an investment to reap dividends, and instant results are rarely part of the deal.

Budgeting Your Bananas

Your marketing budget should be based on your gross annual or projected gross annual revenue. Multi-system/location operators generally need to spend more money on advertising than single-system operators because they have more jobs to fill.

Devote 5% to 25% of gross sales to your marketing budget, depending on your length of time in business. The longer you are in business, the less money you will need to spend in advertising because your word-of-mouth referrals will grow. That is, of course, IF you provide stellar service. Obviously, you cannot afford to spend more than you have. As a rule of thumb, avoid spending more than you can easily carry as a monthly payment until the income starts to flow.

Scott "The Game Master" Faver, owner of The Party Favers with offices in California and Arizona, believes that your investment should be divided among several key areas. "Advertising, public relations, media planning, pricing, sales and customer service are all parts of your comprehensive marketing effort. As you market your company and its services, keep in mind that all the facets must work together to create an effective strategy."

You'll get the maximum return on investment by targeting your advertising messages at the people who are most likely to hire you for your disc jockey services. This is your target market. Whatever methods of advertising you choose, consider them a test. Develop a system for monitoring the results of each medium (cost vs. return).

Each time a potential new client calls, inquire how they heard about your company, and be sure to keep track of the answer in a computer program. Stay with what works best for your company and make alterations accordingly, if an ad or other medium is not providing sufficient return on investment (ROI).

The best measurement of an ad's effectiveness is whether it brings in enough new business to pay for itself at least twice over. It is important to judge media effectiveness not only by the number of inquiries you receive but also by the cost of obtaining those inquiries.

The Secret to Prosperity

Marketing guru Sterling Valentine shares a secret that the highest-paid DJs already know. "You could be the greatest DJ in your area but if people don't know about you, they can't hire you. Marketing and sales – not talent – are the keys to unlocking your unlimited earning potential as a DJ business owner."

You can forget about the forehead advertising and interactive urinal communicator. Guerrillas control the messages that they send. Every time they beat their chest they are communicating a specific and consistent benefit message targeted to their core prospects.

A good look into your mirror ball will reveal whether you are the true guerrilla marketer you'd like to be.

Pole-Vaulting Over Business Obstacles

As DJ business owners, we all face similar challenges in running a profitable enterprise. While the road to success is paved with a few potholes, dead ends and U-turns, there are some tried-and-true methods for negotiating bumpy territory that will ensure mostly "happy trails" along the journey.

This writer searched the country for mobiles who shared their personal stories about obstacles to business success and the solutions they found to overcome them.

OBSTACLE: Developing the entertainment skills necessary to "read" and motivate audiences to dance, and to program and mix music at events.

SOLUTIONS: Become an apprentice and then work for a multi-system operator. Attend a DJ school or training course as well as public speaking, acting and comedy classes. Find a mentor. Read and watch DJ-specific books and videos. The more of these you attempt, the better versed you become in your craft.

Take, for example, British DJ Paul Evans, who used his interactive skills to triumph over a predicament at a "shotgun" wedding reception. "The bride's and groom's families were different religions and they seemed to hate each other," he says. "You could cut the air with a knife, and no one was moving. I played Johnny Lee's 'Looking for Love,' did a couple of mixes and hoped for the best."

Evans, who owns Silver Sound Disc Jockeys in Philadelphia, was shocked and delighted when the dance floor was soon packed. He had the men and women dance down the middle of the dance floor, two at a time, "Stroll" style.

"Mixing the families together broke the ice and the energy that came from the crowd was unbelievable! I could feel all of the hatred disappear and both families seemed very relieved to let it go."

OBSTACLE: Transitioning from being a part-time to a full-time DJ entertainer.

SOLUTIONS: Develop a business plan. Obtain the necessary funding to start and run your business through personal financing or a loan. Join professional trade associations. Attend DJ conventions and networking gatherings. Join online DJ chats. All of these solutions build your business acumen and provide valuable business relationships that can increase your income to a full-time level.

That's what Karl Langford did. Langford, owner of Multiple Choice Disc Jockeys in Long Prairie, MN, lost his 40-hour-a-week day job and was motivated to move full-time into DJing. "Since I'd lost my main source of income I had to act quickly, so I just hit the pavement to promote my services. At first, it wasn't easy to get gigs but eventually my efforts and determination did pay off."

OBSTACLE: Lower-priced DJs in my market.

SOLUTIONS: Create a unique selling proposition (USP) for your services. Be aware that not every prospect is the right fit for your DJ service, so identify your niche market(s). Focus on the type of events you do best to generate referrals and repeat business.

Rocky Bourg, owner of DJ Music by Request in New Orleans, admits that he tends to take it personally when he gets the dreaded I-can-get-a-DJ-for-half-your-price phone call. "I have to consistently remind myself that not everyone who calls is a potential client for my company," he admits. "I am always polite and professional to such callers, understanding that their needs are just not compatible with my services."

OBSTACLE: A slim booking calendar.

SOLUTIONS: Plan and implement a targeted advertising and marketing campaign. Always put on a stellar performance at events. Volunteer your services at charitable events to gain wider exposure.

OBSTACLE: Lack of a comprehensive music library.

SOLUTIONS: Research what is needed based on the market(s) you serve (e.g., weddings, school dances, mitzvahs , etc.). Build a music collection by subscribing to a professional DJ music subscription service, through purchasing compilations, greatest-hits collections and remixes from specialty distributors.

OBSTACLE: Balancing career, family and personal time.

SOLUTION: Recognize that sacrifices have to be made to achieve success. Work hard at staying organized, and make room in your schedule for whomever and whatever are the top priorities. In the end, you can only stretch so far, so don't forget time for yourself to renew those creative juices.

Part-time DJ Ron Keys of Kansas City, MO, says his most frustrating dilemma has nothing to do with capital but rather finding the time to dedicate to his DJ business. "I wish there were more hours in the day," he says, "so I could work on my advertising, sound and lighting systems as well as a number of other things that would allow me to grow my company in a professional manner."

OBSTACLE: Prospects don't return contracts and deposits in a timely manner.

SOLUTION: Clearly state both verbally and in your contract: "The deposit must be received by the due date to guarantee services for your event. Company is holding a tentative reservation until that date. Contracts received after the deposit due date are subject to DJ's availability." Call the prospect if the contract is not received by the due date.

OBSTACLE: Retaining a quality entertainment staff.

SOLUTION: Compensate your DJs well. Show respect and appreciation for their contributions. Provide them with growth opportunities in your company. Always keep staff in the information "loop." Create a business culture that is positive for everyone who works for you.

OBSTACLE: Being a talented DJ but lacking in the business, marketing and sales skills to become a business owner.

SOLUTION: Not everyone is cut out to be a business owner; however, if you think you are, then get education and training in the areas in which you are lacking expertise.

Cheryl Quinlan of Cheryl Q Productions in Florida makes a good point about how important it is to be well-rounded with our skills: "To be successful, both our DJing and business acumen need to be compatible. Someone can be a great DJ with outstanding entertainment abilities and be a crappy business person, or they can be a skilled negotiator and a lousy DJ."

OBSTACLE: Unpleasant surprises at venues.

SOLUTION: Visit a venue that is new to you before an event and scope out its electrical system, and load-in/out location. Meet with management to inquire about in-house policies related to fog machines, confetti launchers and other issues relevant to your performance.

Is there a lesson to be learned from obstacles? Yes, if you think of them as challenges that can be valuable growth opportunities.

Attitude impacts the bottom line and with a positive one nothing is insurmountable. The vast majority of the most successful DJ entertainers, including this writer, experienced their greatest triumphs after their largest personal and/or professional setbacks.

When it comes to overcoming obstacles, perhaps it was Henry Ford who said it best: "Whether you think you can or think you can't, you're right."

Going Multi-Op

DJ Bobby's bookings had grown to the point where he alone could no longer fulfill them. He was tired of losing out on events because he wasn't available for a date and had to refer away business to his competitors.

Bobby realized the timing was probably right for him to go multi-op. He already had three sound systems but he worried about finding other DJs as good as himself. Bobby's quandary was that he had no experience in supervising or training employees. What's more, he had heard that managing DJs is like trying to herd cats, so how in the world would he be able to make this transition smoothly?

He didn't. Bobby recruited a few DJs into his fold and learned how to manage them strictly through trial and error. One guy left after only two months. Eventually, after spending much more time and money than he had anticipated, Bobby finally had a solid team of three and was able to fulfill his event dates. In retrospect, he wished someone had advised him to "look before you leap."

"Going multi-op is like instantly giving birth to quintuplets," says Brian Doyle, co-owner of Denon & Doyle Disc Jockey Company in Concord, CA. "With patience, research and a lot of hard work it can be just as rewarding. If not, you will soon be wishing for the days of bachelorhood."

With that in mind, here are some tools for effectively recruiting and managing your entertainment staff.

Staff Recruitment

Do you want to hire experienced DJs or would you prefer to train someone to entertain "your way"? If you lean toward the latter, then here are some places and means to finding new recruits:

Events: Has a guest at an event ever gotten on the mic and blown you away with his/her talent or personality? Use this type of opportunity to introduce yourself, hand the person one of your business cards and say, "I think you'd make a great DJ!" Also, sometimes servers in restaurants are really actors with a day job. Keep your talent antenna up for big personalities when dining out.

Existing Staff: Offer a $100 bonus as an incentive for current staffers to refer talent to you. Be sure to pay a bonus only if you hire the person and he/she stays with your company for a minimum of six months.

Ads: You can place an ad for free on craigslist.com. Other paid options include your local area entertainment publications and newspapers.

Flyers: Place "Help Wanted" flyers in retail locations that sell pro-audio gear and on the bulletin board in the drama department of local colleges.

Once you've got some applicants to interview, prescreen them over the phone first before meeting with them in person. Anyone who doesn't meet the following basic criteria is probably not a good candidate:

Availability: Is the applicant available on weekends?

Drivers License & Vehicle: It's hard to be a mobile entertainer without a vehicle. Ask if the person has a valid driver's license and a reliable vehicle.

Future Plans: If someone plans to move away in the year, it's hardly worth your time training them.

Health: Pre-existing back or major health problems make it difficult for someone to perform the necessary duties of a mobile DJ.

Personality: If the person on the other end of the phone line comes across as lacking enthusiasm or doesn't have an appealing speaking voice, the odds are they're not going to make a good interactive party host.

Performance Skills: Talent as an actor, singer, dancer, comedian or magician can enhance being a DJ.

Attitude: This may be the most important quality of all. If someone strikes you as an egomaniac or admits to being only interested in the job to make quick money and meet chicks, they probably don't have the attitude or ethics to meet professional standards.

Training

When hiring inexperienced people, provide them with a comprehensive training program that includes a manual. To initiate the new DJ into the business, training should include a combination of lecture; hands-on practice; observation of your other DJs at events; and on-the-job, supervised performance prior to going solo.

Your thorough training agenda should cover all aspects of performance, sequenced in a logical order, as well as your company's policies, procedures, and standards and practices. It is important to have clear and concise standards that apply equally to everyone who works for you.

Consider implementing a probationary period for all new employees. This can also apply to existing ones who have violated company policy.

The use of video can be very useful in training, especially to show performance examples or how to properly set up sound and lighting gear. Show your "newbie" some footage of other DJs performances as well as other "how-to" videos (e.g., party games, interactive dances, etc.).

Provide evaluations a couple of times per year and always be consistent in your words and actions. Praise people when they perform well and give criticism constructively (and privately) when it is needed. Your ability to communicate your expectations effectively with people will be a major factor in your success as a manager.

Internal Customer Service

Remember, you not only have external customers but internal ones as well. Are your employees loyal ambassadors of your company? The best way to turn them into high-ranking diplomats is to compensate your DJs well, show appreciation of and respect for the contributions they make, and provide opportunities for professional growth.

Since most of your employees are likely part-timers, you must provide consistent incentives for them to uphold your company's standards and hard-earned reputation.

To gain buy-in, Missouri-based DJ Nexus tries to make his DJs happy by making their job as easy as possible. "I personally handle 90% of the work that needs to be done for an event," he says. "This includes closing the sale, meeting with the client, scheduling and special music requests. The list goes on and on."

If you think about it, the success of any facet of your business can almost always be traced back to motivated employees. From productivity and profitability to recruiting and retention, hardworking and happy employees lead to a corporate culture that benefits everyone.

Unfortunately, motivating people is far from an exact science. There's no secret formula, no set calculation, no worksheet to fill out. In fact, motivation can be as individual as the people who work for you. One person may be motivated only by money. Another may appreciate recognition at staff meetings for a job well done. Still another may view perks as his/her primary motivation.

As a boss, Brandon Lindsey of Hey! Mr. DJ, Entertainment in Cincinnati, OH, wanted to build loyalty, reliability and friendship among his staffers, and to reward them for their hard work and he came up with some creative ways to do it. "During our monthly meetings I provide food and training," he says. "It's an educational and team-building experience as well as an opportunity for everyone to give input. Once a month my DJs meet up after our events for a late night dinner. We all talk about how our gigs went and I pay the bill. I also throw a Christmas party every year at a local hot spot and pick up the tab for that. It's a chance for us all to socialize and blow off some steam. We always have a great time. I just spent about $1,200 on carts, straps and other tools to make my DJs' jobs easier."

Across the border in Edmonton, Alberta, Canada, Kevin Kirouac, chimes in about the value of tempering friendship with effective leadership. "We treat our guys like friends and respect their suggestions," he says. "And they respond well to criticism when it's warranted. We drive into them that we have a 'chain of command' and 'standard operating procedures' that everyone, even the owners, must follow. All complaints are required to be submitted in writing and signed. The complaint is reviewed by management and then with the employee. A resolution beneficial to all parties is drafted and then implemented."

Getting staff members to represent your company in a positive manner is not impossible, nor is it a "happy accident." It is the result of a carefully planned management approach that is applied successfully.

When it comes to effective management, DJ Steve Rhodes lives by this motto: "A good manager doesn't necessarily have to know how to do anything well, other than find good people that do know how to do things well. When managing people, just never ask them to do something that you wouldn't do yourself."

Celebrate achieving goals and surpassing milestones such as "300 events booked in 2009." Commemorating these accomplishments underscores the value that each person brings to the table.

Study after study has shown that praise and recognition tend to build employee loyalty. People want to feel that what they do makes a difference. Money alone does not do this; personal recognition does.

Compensation

The compensation for DJs ranges from $15 to $300 an hour depending on a variety of factors. With employees or independent contractors, a business owner might consider paying 25-70% of the contract. How much exactly? Here are the primary factors to consider:

- Experience and talent

- Length of service/employment with your company

- Specifically requested by a client

- Type of event
- Travel distance to and from the party
- Number of hours booked
- Event-planning responsibility
- Provided the client lead
- Closed the sale for your company
- A high percentage of past positive client reviews

Additional factors include who provides the transportation, equipment and music for an event. Rate increases should only be awarded for quality performances as determined by Client Satisfaction Surveys and adherence to company standards, policies and procedures.

Most DJ services share the overtime with the entertainer. The MC and/or DJ should be allowed to keep 100% of the gratuities. I recommend adding verbiage to your company contract that states, "Gratuities given to your DJ are made at the client's sole discretion — 10-15% is customary for an excellent performance." Knowing there is a likely tip at the end of a gig can be a strong performance motivator.

Greg Tish, owner of GT Entertainment in Tallahassee, FL, believes he pays his DJs at a higher rate than any other company in his local area. Tish's motivation is simple: "I take care of my people with what they need and they take care of my company every time they go out to an event."

Maximizing Meetings

There is great benefit to holding monthly staff meetings as a vehicle to cross-train your DJs, create camaraderie, brainstorm information and develop action steps toward accomplishing company goals. The more employees know about the goals of your business and how they can contribute to accomplishing them, the more they will be able to contribute.

Create a worthy agenda and stick to it. Keep the gathering to about two hours, and watch the clock. A good facilitator will chart out periods of time for each topic and will help the group decide how best to use the remaining time allotted if an agenda item requires more discussion.

Meetings are work. But that doesn't mean participants can't have fun. Allow joking, small talk, etc. Know when to cut chatter, too, like when no one has focused on the issue at hand for a couple of minutes. Make the environment one in which people are comfortable, both physically and emotionally.

Going multi-op after being a single operator certainly has its share of challenges; however, the reward of being able to take on additional bookings and increase your annual profit may well be worth the trials, tribulations and effort. Here's to your growing pains!

Offering a Money-Back Guarantee

Is offering a money-back guarantee a powerful hot button for getting prospects to buy? You bet it is. Why? Most people want S.E.X. – Security, Essentials and the Xtras of life.

For mobile entertainers, offering a money-back guarantee (MBG) provides security because, for your prospects, it removes risk. To make an MBG work for your business, it must be marketed effectively as well as being backed up with great service and excellent performances.

Most DJs who have an MBG find at least a slight increase in their bookings, and every little bit helps. The amount of new business you will gain from having a service guarantee will almost certainly exceed the amount of money you'll have to shell out to unsatisfied clients.

At Your Service

The important part of any guarantee is not so much that it serves as a marketing tool but that it represents your philosophy regarding customer service. You can think of it as a pledge, promise or commitment. At the heart of a good MBG is a fundamental desire to serve your clients and this is what ultimately builds loyalty in the form of referrals and repeat business.

Your MBG must be a carefully worded conditional offer. Naturally, there may be instances when people abuse your goodwill by taking advantage of your service standards (e.g., a penny-pinching client who overspent on their event and then looks for a bogus excuse to get money back from you); however, most problem situations can be partially or fully remedied if handled with professionalism, sensitivity and timely follow-up.

Steve Hoffman, owner of Good Note DJs in Washington, D.C., avoids the pitfalls of an MBG. "I meet with potential clients in advance to get a sense of whether or not we are on the same wavelength. This keeps me on my toes and discourages me from accepting jobs that aren't a good match. Once I accept someone as a client, I develop a rapport with him or her during the planning phase so if down the road something goes wrong, the client still thinks favorably of me."

Hoffman requires that any client request for money back must be in writing within ten business days after their event and it must include a written explanation of the reason for their dissatisfaction. Has he ever had to give a refund? "There was only one time that a client requested their money back, which I thought was unfair. However, I did honor the terms of my contract and refunded the fee 100%."

If you find yourself refunding more than 5% of your sales to dissatisfied clients, then you have a service or performance problem that needs your immediate attention. In this case, it is worth every penny it costs you to identify and fix the problem before it has a more major impact on your business.

Put Your Money Where Your Mouth Is

"Money Back," "Unconditional," "Iron-Clad," "100%," "Risk-Free," and "Lifetime" are the types of guarantees typically offered. In our business, "A Guaranteed Good Time" has become a popular choice. Whatever your preference of phrasing, make sure the content of your guarantee includes only those items over which you have control. The importance of that last sentence cannot be emphasized strongly enough.

One example of a particularly bold MBG comes from DJ Robert Starkey, who has what he calls a "Making Your Wedding Magical Money Back Guarantee." In it, Starkey makes this gutsy promise to his clients: "If at the end of your wedding you can look me in the eyes and tell me I didn't do a great job, I will refund 100% of your money to you."

I can guess what you're thinking. Has this promise ever come back to bite Starkey in the a$$? "Never! But my guarantee is conditional in that a client must request their money back the same night as their event and before I leave the venue. They must also attend all scheduled consultations and complete at least 90% of the planning form I have given them. These conditions ensure that a client doesn't 'flake out' and do zero planning – and then expect me to meet expectations they haven't expressed."

"Kiwi" Nick Logan from Nites Alive Entertainment in New Zealand prefers to guarantee his standards in writing rather than offer an MBG. Why? "I see a money-back guarantee as a gimmick used by DJs who have nothing else to offer, and no other way of standing out; however, I also don't ask for payment until the day of the event."

Your Service Guarantee

Here are some examples that you can include in your service guarantee. You can customize them to best suit your company and the types of events you do:

- The agenda for your reception will be custom-tailored according to your personal preferences and style and we will give you expert input on how to make it fun and memorable.

- Your MC and DJ will arrive one hour to 90 minutes prior to your guests' arrival to set up and do a sound check with the equipment. They will be ready to start performing on time.

- Your MC will coordinate the reception agenda with the designated facility contact as well as the photographer and videographer.

- The well-maintained professional-quality sound and lighting equipment used at your event will be rack-mounted and neatly cased.

- Your DJ will gladly play the song requests you have indicated on your Event Planner as well as the on-the-spot danceable requests from your guests as selection fits and time permits.

- Your MC and DJ will be dressed in appropriate attire, according to the preference you have indicated on your Wedding Reception Planner.

- Your MC and DJ will play continuous music throughout your event without a break and the volume will be set to appropriate levels during cocktail, meal and dance times.

- Your MC and DJ will not consume alcohol before or during your event.

- All conditions in your Entertainment Agreement will be fulfilled.

Congratulations! Now you've got a Money Back Guarantee perfectly befitting your business, so let your future clients know about it by hanging a poster-size copy in your office. Include your service guarantee on your website and in your client contract. Feature it in your brochure, audio-visual presentation and advertising.

Last but not least, be sure to instruct your DJs on the fine points of your guarantee so they can take pride in working for a company that stands behind its service promise. Getting buy-in from your disc jockeys to perform according to your commitment will pay dividends – guaranteed, or your money back.

Mastering the Art of Follow-Up

Congratulations on being the most talented DJ in your area! You have the best equipment, a fantastic marketing program and you give excellent customer service. So, why are some of your competitors booking more events and making more money than you? How unfair!

Calm down and let's deconstruct the situation. It could be that you are focusing too much on the preparation and performance of events and neglecting to make ample time for sales. If that's the case, does your selling process include follow-up, follow-up, follow-up? This is my favorite memo from the Department of Redundancy Department.

To master the art of follow-up, you must become a persistent persuader of people. If you don't have an effective follow-up system in place then you're likely missing out on new and repeat sales, upsell opportunities and referrals, as well as gaining valuable insight on client satisfaction.

Creating a System

There are several popular general business contact-management programs that do an outstanding job of keeping track of leads and records, reminding you of appointments, and scheduling follow-up contact dates.

Industry-specific programs include DJ Intelligence, DJ Webmin, Gigbuilder and DJ Manager.

Using an email auto-responder service will allow you to send automatic responses to inquiries with pre-specified messages on the dates and at the times you choose. You must set up your system in a manner that allows you to contact each lead, prospect or client individually, multiple times and at set intervals, with pre-written messages sent personally to them.

Once your system is created, it's important to carefully track each step of your follow-up in order to determine how it's working. You'll want to know exactly what you did that motivated a prospect to book you, purchase a larger package, or a client to hire you again and/or refer you others. Be sure to ask your clients their reasons why as well as how you can improve your services – and keep track of the responses.

Here's some advice from Boston-based DJ Kristin Korpos, who thinks of the sales process as a continuous experiment. She takes copious notes in order to know what works and what doesn't for her business. "By effectively documenting who I have talked to, when I have talked to them and what has been said, I can pull up that information and set up my calls to prospective clients with whom I am trying to close, as well as current and prior clients."

Paying attention to what works best will allow you to tweak your efforts for continually greater results. While the process may sound tedious, it's the only way to make sure your system is running like a finely oiled machine.

Follow Through on Your Follow-up

New York-based Stephanie and Jeff Padova, owners of The DJ Solution, use email, e-Newsletters, snail mail and telephone calls to communicate with clients. "We send information that includes event planning details and timelines, song suggestions, tips for planning a wedding and even demos of acoustic guitar instrumentals available for their event," says Stephanie. "For a personal touch, we also include a photograph of ourselves in our email signature."

Some other excellent reasons to communicate include sending:

- Your entertainment marketing package.

- An announcement of a limited-time offer, new product or service you are offering.

- Helpful information of interest to your target audience.

- A Client Satisfaction Survey after an event.

- A thank-you letter following an event along with a postcard about the other services your business offers.

- A card thanking someone for their business or referral or for a birthday, anniversary or holiday (SendOutCards.com can help you put a system in place).

- A request to satisfied clients and other contacts for referrals, which may include incentives such as promotional items, movie tickets or gift certificates. If sending a letter, be sure to include a few business cards.

The Padovas also market to other wedding professionals to maximize referral opportunities from them. "We send a postcard bearing our photo to every vendor we work with as a thank-you," says Jeff. "It makes a great impression and reminds them of who we are. Because our photo is on the card, we think people hang on to it and remember us."

Tom "Fatman" French, owner of Fatman Entertainment in Vacaville, CA, has three major goals for his follow-up system: "First, to get feedback that will better my performance; second, to keep my name in front of customers; and third, to generate referrals by asking for them."

French's business focus is on weddings, and he's devised a clever way to be remembered by his past clients. "For a couple's first anniversary, I send them a restaurant gift card along with a few business cards and I once again ask for referrals," he says. "I also remind them to break out the wine I gave them as a thank-you gift. This is a specially engraved bottle that I present at the reception while the bride and groom are eating. I suggest to them that they save it for a special toast on their first anniversary."

Follow-up provides opportunities for new interactions, shows a high level of commitment, and regularly reminds folks about your DJ service, which helps to create top-of-mind awareness. So, continue building rapport with your prospects, former clients and networking contacts. This represents a down payment on your future. The price is effort, discipline and organization.

Korpos reminds us that when you follow up effectively you present yourself as a professional. "For prospective clients it shows them that you are concerned about their needs and that you are attentive. This attentiveness means more bookings and more satisfied clients in the long run."

True masters of follow-up are persistent. And this stick-to-itiveness is incredibly persuasive. After a while, if you continue to remind people of what you offer and how they can benefit from it, they will give you a chance to prove it.

As the late motivational author and speaker Earl Nightingale put it, "Luck is what happens when preparedness meets opportunity."

Stacy with some DJ buddies: Keith Alan, Jason Jani, Ray Martinez, Grand Master Gee of the Sugarhill Gang, Ken Heath and Matt Peterson.

Stacy with more DJ buddies: Sean "Big Daddy" McKee, Johnny K, Marcello Pedalino and Dennis Hampson. Group shot includes: Mike Handy, Stacy Zemon, Ray Martinez, Johnny K, Keith "K.C." KoKoruz, Jeff Greene, Mark Klatskin and George Whitehouse.

Excellent business card examples from Brian Dowdle of Dowdle Design.
The logo is from Bob Carpenter of Main Event Weddings.

International DJ Expo "DJ of the Year" competition opener and closer, Johnny K (Photo courtesy, Elite Entertainment). 2009 winner, Steve Moody.

Excellent examples of totally different kinds of business cards from Jason Jani of Sound Connection Entertainment and Christian Jackson of Pump It Up DJ!

An elegant matching marketing set from Joe and Heather Staniszewski of JBS Entertainment.

2009 International DJ Expo "DJ of the Year" competition judges: Sid Vanderpool, John Rozz, Jeffrey Craig, Ray Martinez, Stacy Zemon and Marcello Pedalino. A beautiful wedding set-up from Dave Schoonover of TNG Digital DJ Services.

A beautiful set-up and front board from Steve Cie Entertainment.
Producer of the International DJ Expo and owner of Elite Entertainment,
Mike Walter, having fun a bride and her bridesmaids.

Excellent logo examples from Betsy Fisher, M.Ed. of Betsy Fischer's Groove Lounge and Dave Schoonover of TNG Digital DJ Services.

Excellent examples of a wedding website home page from Wayde West of Your Wedding Entertainment and a bridal fair set-up from Wes Flint of DJ Wes' Mobile DJ Service.

A photo of and logos from Jason Jani of Sound Connection Entertainment and Johnny K of Pure Energy Entertainment and Johnny K Entertainment.

Excellent examples of a wedding set-up from Ron Montgomery of Atomic Sound Entertainment and a New Year's Eve set-up from Will Curran of Arizona Pro DJs.

Excellent examples of creative staff photos at unique locations from Silver Sound Entertainment and Elite Entertainment.

Veteran lady DJ entertainers, Betsy Fischer, M.Ed., Charlene Burg and Randi Rae.

A great brochure from Marc Sparks of MS Soundworks, showcasing the
Jambulance Mobile Entertainment Center. Stacy Zemon's DJ business card

A high-tech mobile rig from Bob Carpenter of Main Event Weddings. Chuck Lehnhard from Maui Mobile Music shows that there is no escaping the Mummy Wrap.

An elegant set-up from Nate Horowitz of New Vibe Entertainment. The Beat Street Dance & Party Room from Bobby Morganstein Productions.

2009 Beat Street Dance & Party Room

Why It Pays to Be Charitable

The idea that giving makes you rich is a lovely sentiment to be sure but it's quite backward-sounding to the average businessperson. You obviously have to be prosperous before you can give away your services for free or at a significantly reduced rate to charity, right?

Well, actually, no. There is quite a bit of research that supports the idea that behaving generously actually stimulates prosperity – and this is true for individuals, businesses, communities and nations. Being charitable, it seems, really can make you rich.

Why Giving is Good for Us

Both psychologists and neuroscientists have identified several ways that giving makes us more effective and successful. Helping others not only makes us feel good about ourselves, but it can also increase our physical well-being.

- Research by the University of Oregon has found that volunteerism stimulates the parts of the brain that are associated with meeting basic needs, which suggests to researchers that our brains know that giving is good for us.

- A study by Cornell University found that volunteering increases a person's energy, sense of mastery over life and self-esteem.

- Studies have demonstrated that positive feelings about yourself can actually strengthen and enhance your immune system.

- Research has shown that people are often elevated by others into positions of leadership after they are witnessed behaving charitably.

So, is achieving wealth, health or becoming a leader the primary reason to give or rather a byproduct of being generous? This writer asked some mobiles about their motivation, and here's what they had to say.

Cap Capello of Saratoga, NY, has a very good reason to donate his time and talents to charity. His daughter has been institutionalized since birth due to severe physical and mental birth defects. Capello channels his desire to make a difference by performing several times a year for both the Center for The Disabled and the Association of Retarded Citizens. "I've contributed my mobile DJ services to them for the past twenty years," he says. "Over the course of this time I have become good friends with the staff and the patients. The staff are angels and the patients are so filled with love, they are positively the best audience anyone could dream of performing for. If I weren't asked to entertain for these fine organizations, I would call them and beg to do so."

Ever the consummate professional, Capello still uses a no-charge contract to ensure his liability coverage is in place and that out-of-pocket expenses can be deducted and proven for tax purposes. Capello steadfastly maintains his business policies in strict accordance with the advice from his attorney and CPA.

For Northern New Jersey's DJ Teddy Bear, the American Cancer Society's Relay For Life is an annual event on his calendar. The same goes for California's Ezra Mendoza of Rhythm & Rhapsody, who also donates his services to Ronald McDonald House. "I had the unfortunate experience of being a guest there when my son was in the hospital for an extended period of time," says Mendoza, "And I have also lost some very important people in my life from 'The Big 'C'.'"

Mendoza challenges his clients to join him in giving. "I run a discount program," he says, "Whereby if my client writes a check up to $100 made out directly to the charity, I will match that amount in any entertainment package $700 and over. I also send part of the proceeds of sales from my company-branded merchandise to Ronald McDonald House."

Popular Party DJs' Charlene Burg's friend was a victim of a double-murder during her senior year in high school. The family of one of the victims wanted to do something positive in remembrance of their daughter, so they started a foundation for battered and homeless women. Burg knew immediately that she wanted to join the cause to help other women from being abused or killed, and keep their spirits alive to the public. "I offered my services to assist with fundraising in memory of my friend," says Burg. "The first year we raised $50,000, and we have raised an additional $750,000 over the past twenty-five years. Various artists have attended this event, such as Sissy Houston [Whitney's musical mother]. I'm so glad to be part of such a wonderful cause and would never give it up for the world."

Brand Aid

Not only do people feel a greater sense of purpose when expressing their abundance through giving but philanthropy also serves as a key way to create a positive corporate image. It can have a huge impact on branding because today's consumers are more conscious than ever before about the companies they buy from and are looking for more meaning in their purchases.

Donating your services or offering them at a reduced rate to charity is also a very good way to build your company's reputation and client roster. Here are three ways to do it:

1. Prospects can often be invited to a charitable event, giving them a unique opportunity to see your live performance, which is something that is usually not advisable with private functions.

2. You can include your charitable activities on your company's website and marketing materials.

3. In lieu of a cash payment for a charitable event, you can request an exchange in which you provide the entertainment and the charity features your company's ad or information in all of their marketing, advertising and publicity for the event in which you are performing.

If you don't have a personal reason for choosing a particular charity and want to check out different options, here are a few sites that will make your task easy: guidestar.org, give.org, charitynavigator.org, and ebaygivingworks.com.

Once you decide upon a few possibilities, contact the charity's local branch in your community and find out if they already have enough annual events established to meet their financial needs. If not, then you have an opportunity to establish a fundraiser for them.

It is important to understand that your DJ services are not tax deductible, even when providing event entertainment for a charitable, religious, educational, scientific, literary, or prevention of cruelty to children or animals organization. However, your out-of-pocket expenses, such as mileage, parking fees, tolls, material expenses (supplies), cost of goods (merchandise distributed), payroll, dry cleaning, repairs, and reasonable expenses for meals and lodging are tax deductible. Consult IRS Publication 526 or your accountant for more details.

The one who ends up getting the most from giving may, ultimately, be the Good Samaritan. It really does pay to be a DJ do-gooder because as famed motivational speaker Tony Robbins puts it, "Only those who have learned the power of sincere and selfless contribution experience life's deepest joy: true fulfillment. It's not what we get but who we become and what we contribute that gives meaning to our lives."

Ten Ways to Keep Your DJs Happy

After meeting socially on several occasions, DJ Mike asked Lenny to join his multi-system mobile entertainment operation. Mike thought that Lenny, a novice who had bought some audio gear and practiced with it at home and at house parties, had "the right stuff" to succeed as a disc jockey, and so Mike assumed the task of molding him into the kind of entertainer who would do a great job representing his business.

Mike spent countless hours over the course of a year training his "newbie" on all aspects of performance and customer service. Lenny came along quickly, graduating from roadie to DJ – and then to a full-fledged MC. As a savvy business owner, Mike even had Lenny sign a non-compete agreement so he could rest assured that his new recruit would stay with his company and not try to strike out on his own.

Needless to say, Mike was stunned, hurt, disappointed and angry when, after only two years, Lenny left to start his own mobile entertainment company. Mike felt robbed of his investment and the last thing in the world he needed was another competitor in his area.

Mike took Lenny to court over the non-compete agreement, but the judge ruled in Lenny's favor because the contract wasn't worded specifically enough to legally keep Lenny from leaving Mike's business and starting his own.

Where did DJ Mike go wrong? If this sad tale has happened to you or you fear it might – relax and listen up. This writer has some good advice on ways to turn your DJs into loyal, long-term, highly motivated ambassadors for your company. Here are some creative ideas to get you started:

1. Pay your DJs well and fairly. Go out of your way to praise them when they are doing a great job. Give biannual rate increases and every reason you can think of to stay and be happy working for your company.

2. Help your DJs get tipped. You can do this by teaching them tricks of the trade such as providing the groom

with a rose to give to the bride, turning down the meal, helping to wait on the head table, releasing the tables for the buffet line and looking for any opportunity to go the extra mile with customer service. Your DJs will be grateful to have earned the extra $50 to $100 or more per gig, and this perk didn't cost you anything.

3. Let your DJs keep their overtime money. This should apply to overtime requested by a client at an event, not in advance. It is a great incentive for an employee to know that he or she gets to keep 100% of the dividends from a jammin' party at which a happy client asks him or her to extend the playing time.

4. Launch an employee recognition program. Provide $50 to $100 cash-value gift cards to those who receive "X" number of high ratings from Client Satisfaction Surveys. Praise a winning employee publicly in front of the other DJs at your monthly employee meeting while presenting him or her with a hand-written greeting card from you with the gift card tucked inside.

5. Provide more frequent work for your top performers. Seniority is a good thing because it means a DJ has been with your company for some time; however, in our business no one gets to rest on their laurels. So, motivate your employees to continue striving for their best by giving your consistently top performers first dibs on new gigs.

6. Offer a $100 bonus for new DJ referrals. The bonus should be available to all of your staffers, and it is best to give it only if you hire the person and he/she stays with your company for at least six months.

7. Create a first-class company image and a positive work environment. Your staff will be proud to be associated with a company that has an excellent reputation and commands top dollar for its services. Set an example as a strong yet understanding leader. Share your company's triumphs with your DJs at monthly meetings. Such gatherings help your employees bond with one another,

offer an opportunity for you to publicly acknowledge people and hand out awards, as well as being an excellent time for your DJs to share their successes and challenges in order to learn from one another.

8. Provide rate increases based on positive client evaluations as well as adherence to your company's standards, policies and procedures. A potential pay raise is an excellent incentive for your DJs to continually want to better their best. For those who slack off, however, pay decreases can also be made. Consider starting a newbie at 25% of the gross income for a gig and topping out at 70% (which should take at least a few years to reach).

9. Provide a training program for new DJs. To initiate the newcomer into your business, have regular training sessions that include a combination of lecture, hands-on-practice, observation with your other DJs at events and on-the-job supervised performance prior to going solo. Your thorough training agenda should cover all aspects of performance sequenced in a logical order, as well as your company's policies, procedures and standards – all set forth in a comprehensive training manual.

10. Provide quality equipment and a comprehensive music library for your DJs if that is how your company operates. When you provide your staff with all of the tools necessary to perform well, you're helping them to succeed. When people are succeeding at a job, they rarely feel the need to look elsewhere.

Remember your internal customers – your staff. The best way to attract and retain the best people is to compensate them well, show appreciation for the contributions they make and provide ongoing opportunities for professional and financial growth. These actions are nearly guaranteed to make them happy.

From performance and productivity to accountability and retention – talented, motivated and hardworking staffers lead to increased profitability and longevity for your business. And that should make YOU very happy!

The Path to Prosperity - An Inside Job

Many of us got into DJing because we thought it would be a fun and rewarding way to make money. When you first got into the business, did you think about what it would take to be successful?

While success can certainly be measured in terms of distance traveled, perhaps it's time to really define what this word means to you and what true prosperity is all about. Here's a "magic" formula to help you with this process:

1. Commit to your success and believe that you deserve it.

2. Write down your S.M.A.R.T. (Specific, Measurable, Achievable, Realistic and Timely) goals and create an action plan.

3. Imagine accomplishing your goals and act as if you've already achieved them.

4. Secure at least one mentor and if desired, a spiritual advisor to help you in achieving your goals.

5. Follow your action plan on a daily basis and remove all obstacles that stand in your way.

6. Let your heart, not your ego, be your guide.

7. Be honest, patient, persistent and generous in your thoughts, words and actions.

8. Help others to have what you want for yourself.

9. Find ways to "recharge your batteries" by participating in activities that motivate, relax and inspire you. Eating healthfully and getting regular exercise will also help keep you in peak physical condition.

Mike Walter, owner of Elite Entertainment in Eatontown, NJ, visualizes achieving his goals and acts as if he has already reached them. He has used this philosophy to successfully train for several New York City marathons and it has been his philosophy in business for years. "We are all ultimately responsible for whether we succeed at achieving a goal – or not," he says. "I know that the only thing that can stand in my way is my own lack of confidence. Nothing can stop me from being successful except my belief in my own limitations!"

Prosperity Defined

Our society tends to define success based on outer "trappings," such as how much money we make, the size of our house or the type of car we drive.

There is, however, another way to view your accomplishments. Try focusing on the inner experience of life in terms of how much joy and satisfaction you feel, especially if you have had to overcome difficult obstacles. Perhaps the most useful definition of achievement centers on the continued expansion of happiness and the realization of worthy goals.

"Don't let anyone else make the rules for your happiness," says Idaho-based DJ Sid Vanderpool. "Often it's a balance of family life, personal achievement and doing good for people. Don't let others' 'shoulds' and 'musts' govern your choices. Make up your own mind to set the course for your life."

Successful people understand that there is no such thing as failure, only mistakes from which they can learn. They are persistent, dedicated risk-takers with an unwavering belief in themselves and what they are doing. They aim high, learn quickly from their experiences, are action-oriented and thrive on challenges.

Frank Garcia, owner of Mainline Pro Lighting & Sound and the New York DJ Entertainment School in Flushing, NY, believes that the way to achieve your wildest dreams is to study, absorb, and work hard until the results come. "In the DJ business, perseverance is always the key to success. However, you also need to have a passion for music, the talent to play it well and the ability to stay open-minded."

Wealth is not limited to money. Prosperity can appear in ways we don't recognize and therefore fail to acknowledge. You can wish you were wealthy without realizing the riches that are already present in your life. True affluence also manifests as an abundance of good relationships, health and talent as well as qualities of character such as compassion, generosity and forgiveness.

By letting go of fixed ideas about prosperity, you empower yourself to start enjoying the many levels of it that already surround you.

Get Real with Yourself

Perhaps you have financial security issues, regardless of how much money you have. Or maybe you're holding onto an idea of what prosperity would be for you based upon some vague idea. How much money would it take for you to feel wealthy? $50,000? $100,000? $1 million? More?

It is important to understand that financial security is a feeling that comes from inside you and is not based on an outside source. By taking an honest and detailed personal and monetary inventory, you can realistically assess values as well as your debts, income potential and risk quotient.

Now you are ready to create an action plan for what you want to achieve and how you will get there. Being honest with yourself will allow you to make conscious choices about constructive changes you may need to make in your outlook, attitude, spending, saving and revenue generation.

An important aspect of building an experience of wealth in your life is to put some of your income aside in a savings account. It may seem uncomfortable if you are struggling to pay your bills, but knowing that you are building a "nest egg" can give you a real feeling of abundance. It's kind of like paying yourself first before anyone else to whom you owe money.

If you do have debt, be sure to pay back some amount on a regular basis, preferably monthly, no matter how small. You are constructing a mindset that demonstrates to yourself and others that you can manage material wealth.

Keep the Passion Alive

It is valuable to not only focus on a goal or destination but to also enjoy the journey involved with getting there. Keeping the money flowing and the passion alive in doing the "same old, same old" every weekend requires a change in your attitude and actions.

For example, have you considered becoming a full-service entertainment company by offering photography, video, sound reinforcement and other services and products as upsells? How about creating a targeted advertising and marketing campaign to get your telephone ringing more often.

I Have a Dream

Wanting a big house, a luxury car or a million dollars in the bank is fine, but the really important question is, "Are you willing to pay the price for your dreams?"

It may sound simple, even obvious, but when you're truly committed to achieving your goals, giving up isn't even an option. You must be willing to do whatever it takes to make them happen.

If you love being a DJ and focus on service, financial rewards will naturally follow. Your true motivation must be on what and how you contribute. Monetary returns are always the secondary outcome of serving clients well.

Famed author Norman Vincent Peale offers these words of wisdom for achieving abundant success: "Formulate and stamp indelibly on your mind a mental picture of yourself as succeeding. Hold this picture tenaciously. Never permit it to fade. Your mind will seek to develop the picture. Do not build up obstacles in your imagination."

As a professional entertainer, you have an extraordinary opportunity to motivate and energize thousands of people each year. You have been gifted with the power to positively affect the audiences you entertain through your every word and action, as indelible impressions in their hearts and minds, in the moment, and for years to come.

And that, my friends, is true prosperity. Here's to striking it rich!

Closing the Sale

Learning to be a great salesperson is crucial if you want to earn top dollar as a mobile entertainer. Fortunately, there are many great resources that can assist you, such as books, DVDs, magazines, trade shows and DJ associations.

Once you've got some practical knowledge "under your belt," it's time to use it in real-life situations. Let's deconstruct a typical phone call from a prospect.

Qualify Your Caller

Before spending a great deal of time talking with someone, qualify them with a few key questions. There is no need to sell your services unless you have the date available and the expertise in that type of event, and the person you are speaking with has the authority to hire you as well as the ability to pay your asking price. So, begin by asking what date and venue they have in mind and whether the person on the phone will be the only one involved in the decision.

If he/she does not meet this standard, be polite but suggest they call again if the date changes. If there is another decision maker involved, try to set up a conversation with both parties.

People invariably want to know your price before they understand the value you offer. Quoting prices is meaningless until potential clients can put the cost into the context of the benefits they will receive.

New England-based Mark Ashe of Marx Entertainment doesn't bother with price shoppers from advertising media such as phone books or newspaper advertising. "The more solid prospects come from bridal shows, referrals and people who have already seen you perform. These folks are much more apt to appreciate your value."

The best types of prospects truly are people who have already seen you perform and those that come from referrals. It's much easier to close a sale when someone is already predisposed to hire you, and the qualifying process should only take a short while.

If your website has a price quote generator feature that a prospect has already seen and the person contacts you to book your services, you will likely not have to haggle over prices.

Mitch Canter finds it difficult to explain the benefits of his Cherry Hill, NJ-based DJ service without at least having phone contact. "Many of my inquiries come via email, and many prospects only leave email addresses for a response. To adapt to this situation, I respond in an email with the requested price quote and information about our services as well as providing selected links to our website for further details. Follow-up contact on my part often generates the necessary conversation to differentiate my company's services from others."

If you have correctly priced your DJ services and are selling effectively, you should convert approximately 75% of inquiries into bookings. If your closing percentage is higher than this amount, your prices are probably too low. If you are closing less than this percentage, either your prices are too high or your sales skills need improvement.

Show Off Your Assets

You must demonstrate that the value of your services is greater then their cost. Here are some tips that will help you effectively present your assets:

Ask lots of questions: This will allow you to flush out the prospect's concerns, wants and needs so you know how to proceed with your presentation.

Appeal to a prospect's emotions (positive and negative): They fear having an event ruined by an inexperienced DJ who arrives late in improper attire, has lousy equipment and a small music selection. Prospects are seeking the emotional rewards of fun, joy and happiness. They want to know they made the right decision and that others will validate their choice of entertainment.

Make your presentation in a clear and organized manner: Use a combination of "show and tell." Show a prospect your DVD and tell him or her about the features, benefits and value of your services and products. If you do a good job of this, you can overcome many or all of the prospect's objections before they are verbalized.

Demonstrate Value: A prospect is not paying $900 for four hours of DJ services at an event. He/she is investing this amount in exceptional entertainment and quality assurance that comes with booking your services. The $900 includes the hours you spend in pre-planning consultations, travel, equipment setup/breakdown, and entertaining.

Use an assumptive closing technique: All of your words and actions should convey as sense of confidence that you are the right choice of entertainers and that you will get the booking. At the end of your presentation, pull out your contract and close the sale.

Handling Objections

If your prospective client needs to think about engaging your services, there is a strong possibility that you have not adequately addressed his/her objections. An essential part of your job as a salesperson is to scope out what those objections are and address them to the prospect's satisfaction to obtain a booking. "We live in a day and age when the dynamics of sales have changed considerably," says Ashe. "While the client feels they are more in the driver's seat than ever before, DJs still have the opportunity to push the sale because of a demanding day or simply to fill a slow day. Offering extras to the client doesn't cost money out of your pocket, but it does offer a boatload of value to the customer."

Canter adds some additional insight on the subject. "If I can meet personally with a prospect, most of the time I book the event. When someone tells me 'I need to think about it,' this is my clue that I should ask more questions to determine what their points of objection are, and supply satisfactory answers to those points."

DJ Flip works with two other companies besides his own, and divides his time between Orlando, Florida and New Jersey. "In my experience, DJs have the best chance of being hired when prospective clients have already seen them in action. A website or a referral is nice but doing public events where someone can come see you or having a great DVD of your performance to show is the best way to go."

Providing prospective clients with a sense of security is a large factor in the success of your sales efforts. Provide compelling peace-of-mind reasons to hire you, such as providing on-site backup equipment, liability and property insurances, membership in a professional DJ organization, client testimonials, free party-planning services and a money-back guarantee.

Close the Deal

People tend to procrastinate after they decide to buy something if they don't make the purchase immediately, because as time passes, other things distract them. You can avoid losing some of these sales by rewarding customers for taking immediate action (e.g., you could offer a discounted price or a special bonus such as a lighting package for booking you before a specific deadline).

When making a purchasing decision, people want to be sure they're going to get the absolute best return on their investment. Providing authentic testimonials and a money-back guarantee are great ways to dissolve skepticism and fear.

DJ Flip believes in proving his value to prospects and giving them exactly what they want. As an in-demand DJ, he tries to persuade a potential client to book immediately. "When someone tells me they want to engage my services, I explain that unless they lock down the date of their event with a contract, they could end up losing it because of high demand. When a person understands this, they tend not to procrastinate on making a commitment."

Keep Them Coming Back

The greatest source of continued revenue and the fastest way to increase profits is through repeat customers. All promotions should be aimed right from the beginning at not only attracting new clients but in keeping them around.

Obtaining new clients is the most expensive aspect of business. Continued selling to existing ones is the most profitable.

Past clients are the most important source for new bookings through the business they personally generate as well as through the marketing they do for you by telling friends about your services. With a strong roster of satisfied customers, you can then afford to put more energy and assets into attracting new customers.

Ashe says the value of this can't be emphasized enough. "Sometimes you don't realize how important past clients are until you do 10 repeat parties for a family or 15 repeat school dances, or a corporation wants you to do events for their other divisions in different states. It sometimes takes a long time for a DJ to realize that this is a word-of-mouth business and you really need to focus on that!"

Dazzling Audio-Visual Presentations

Looking to "WOW" your prospects with an audio-visual sales presentation that sizzles? It's not that hard to accomplish once you know the winning formula. A great presentation will highlight the features and benefits of your DJ service in a manner that flows in a logical order. The components can include video, photographs, PowerPoint, audio, and special effects.

Whether you make presentations at in-person meetings, display video on your website, youtube.com and vimeo.com or mail out DVDs to prospects, the production you create needs to tell a compelling, informative, moving and exciting story about your company. For maximum impact, it is best to create a different production for every market your company targets (e.g., weddings, corporate, mitzvahs).

Steps to Producing Powerful Presentations

Step 1: Create an outline. Make separate lists of topics that need to be addressed for each of your markets then rank the topics in order of importance. For each topic, create a list of features and benefits. Your content should include information that your audience will both understand and find emotionally appealing.

Step 2: Keep it short and simple. Five to ten minutes in length should suffice. Simplicity takes forethought and planning about what to include and what can be left out. Tell your future client what he/she will receive by booking your company. Demonstrate how your services address your prospect's fears and solve their problems. It's powerful to include testimonials as well. Major points to consider including in your presentation are:

- Your company's name and logo

- Footage from events

- The products/services you offer

- How you solve clients' concerns and fears

- Distinctions between you and your competitors

- Power Partnerships (e.g., photography, videography, and limousine service providers)

Music and sounds you include should be powerful and memorable. The song selections you include should match the type of event(s) you are showcasing visually. Music can also help you transition from one point to another (e.g., segueing from classical music to dance music for a wedding prospect). Avoid cheesy and superfluous sound effects.

Step 3: Don't overwhelm your audience with techno-fluff. Use a variety of dissolves, wipes and professional-looking transitions to move from one point or scene to another throughout your entire production. Don't overdo it with so many special effects that it distracts from the points you are making.

Step 4: Make sure your script is well-written with proper grammar. It may be a good idea to hire a professional copywriter to help you with this.

Step 5: Before declaring your production complete, run it past your staff, DJs, friends or family members. To pass the "test," your presentation must thoroughly and memorably tell your story. The better job you do with this, the fewer unanswered questions a prospect will have at the end of watching the production.

This writer asked some mobiles who have created effective productions to share what they did and the reasoning behind it. Here's what they had to say:

And Now Our Feature Presentation

Three-time "DJ of the Year" winner Marcello Pedalino features four-minute wedding and Bar Mitzvah videos on his website, mmpentertainment.com. He describes them this way. "The purpose behind the 'short feature' style of our promo videos is to show originality, empathy and demographic preference. For weddings, we want a bride to feel like she is watching a movie trailer for an Oscar-nominated film. Our videos feature footage from my personal wedding ceremony and reception because I want a bride to feel comfortable that I understand the substantial investment and extensive logistics necessary to execute her once-in-a-lifetime experience."

After speaking with clients who were converted from prospects during the sales process, many commented to Pedalino that the video accomplished the desired effect. Mission accomplished.

Michigan's Mark Evans showcases video samples of his DJ work in action on his website, djmarke.com. The four clips focus on weddings and include the Centerpiece Giveaway, Anniversary Dance, Bride & Groom's First Dance, and Cotton Eyed Joe Dance. Evans has also included a video montage of various events.

This subtle sales method has helped him lock in many bookings because before meeting with clients, they had already watched the videos and were impressed with his entertainment style. Evans' advice to DJs who want to create something similar for their websites? "Keep the video(s) short and to the point, and focus on the DJ in action rather than the gear. Ask a videographer you like working with to shoot you at events with his/her professional quality equipment. You may also be able to make an arrangement with that person to put together a montage for your company. Many videographers will do this in exchange for credit on your website because it gives them more exposure and leads for their work."

Kevin Nichols, Owner of DKH Entertainment Group in Macon, GA, uses a different tactic by showing PowerPoint slides intermittently throughout a sales presentation. He breaks down his presentation into five main features: Music, Master of Ceremonies, Entertainment, Planning, and Coordination. "My visuals include various pictures of sound and lighting setups ranging from wild to elegant. I also include pictures of me in different suit and tux ensembles. My intention is that something in the mix will appeal to every prospect. I also include charts to get major points across. You only have one chance to make a first impression, so make it a good one."

A little forethought goes a long way toward maximizing a positive outcome with client meetings. Jason Jani, owner of NJ's Sound Connection Entertainment, sets a positive example. "Every time I am booked in a new venue, I take pictures of my sound and lighting rig. This way I can show a prospect how attractive and professional my system will look set up in the room where their event is being held. People are usually very impressed. Over time, I have gathered pictures from most of the venues in the central and northern part of the state. I also have a blog in which I talk about the events and bridal shows that SCE does."

For sales presentations, Jani also incorporates raw DVD footage that includes an introduction to his company, his business philosophy, and services offered, including music, lights and video. This is followed by a closing.

Jani shows the DVD after first listening to potential client to understand what they are looking for and explaining a bit about himself and his company. He says that by using these techniques, he has been very successful in converting prospects into clients (soundconnectionentertainment.com).

Adding a dazzling audio-visual presentation to the way your company handles sales could turn out to be a cash cow that pays dividends. So give it the love it deserves and then milk it for all it's worth!

Hooking Holiday Clients

The winter holidays are a big gift for savvy DJs who know how to tap into seasonal spending spikes. If you're on the frenzied front lines of the battle for bookings, advance planning is essential for winning sales and raising your company's visibility.

To stand out from the crowd, your holiday promotions must incorporate strong incentives. Make sure they meet or beat what's offered by your competitors to avoid a "ho-hum" reaction from potential and repeat clients.

Add Value – Not Discounts

John Mixon, owner of the Milton, DE-based Salt & Light Entertainment, believes in adding value without compromising his fee. He offers two excellent examples. "We offer free 'Party Photography,' which captures the fun and spontaneity of a client's event through digital photos. This involves taking candid snapshots, then uploading them to Photobucket or another free site where partygoers can later obtain them. Visitors can either save the pics on their computers, print them out, or buy prints from the site. Who wouldn't want a professional photographer at their event for free?"

When necessary to close a deal, Mixon ups the ante even further. Here's his spin. "I tell the prospect that we are introducing a new 'Special Effects Dance Lighting' package for the upcoming year, which has a value of $???. For a limited time this holiday season, we are offering this package at no additional charge in order to obtain client feedback."

Mixon assures his prospect that Salt & Light Entertainment only uses professional, not "cheesy," lighting products. He also explains the value of a light show, which is to create a festive mood that encourages people to dance."

Spread Some Good Cheer

The winter holidays afford you the opportunity to show your gratitude and stay connected to your local community. You could sponsor meals for the homeless, for example. Why not enlist other businesses to join you, and share your story with the local media to aid your cause.

It's also a good time of year to say "thank you" to your clients and VIP associates by hosting a holiday party at an elegant venue where your company regularly entertains. Be sure to invite pending clients and prospects to the shindig, as well.

Ask complementary small businesses with whom you work (e.g., photography and video services) to co-host the event with you. This will keep the costs down and the number of guests up, which always looks more impressive.

In addition to providing music and showcasing your company's MCs, be sure to provide giveaways such as free digital photos in frames and festive holiday party props. People are sure to love live, big-screen video candid shots of the party's attendees. Adding a photo booth, Game Show Mania, Text Live, and holiday-related party games will ensure a truly unforgettable event. In the refreshment category, you could team up with the venue's chef or a local gourmet caterer to offer appetizers and baked-goods delectables. The take-away goodie bags should include brochures from the hosting companies, flyers with all of your holiday specials, promotional items, and other articles such as boxed chocolates, scented candles, personal care delights, etc.

Demonstrating the spirit of giving through year-long volunteerism, Memphis, TN-based Wes Flint, owner of DJ Wes' Mobile DJ Service, shares how his efforts pay off at holiday time. "A few times during the year I provide my company's services at no charge to my local Chamber of Commerce, as well as to the American Liver Foundation and the American Cancer Society's 'Relay For Life' fund-raising events."

Wes believes that by giving back to his community, he has made a memorable impact that brings new and repeat business his way. In addition, he keeps his face in front of other business owners by attending monthly Chamber luncheons to maximize his networking opportunities. "I make sure to shake hands and give out business cards at every meeting. Starting around the September-October time frame, I begin reminding people, especially previous clients, that it's time to book their holiday parties."

Spice Up Seasonal Sales

The holiday season is a great time to engage in efforts that will enhance your company's image and express your appreciation. Try one of these four ideas to foster goodwill and increase sales for your DJ service:

1. Send personalized holiday cards. The VIPs to your business are sure to appreciate receiving one that includes a photo of your staff along with a poignant thought that expresses the sentiments of the season.

2. Donate a portion of your proceeds. The holiday season is a terrific time to demonstrate that your company has heart. Allow clients who book your services between November and January to choose from a list of several national charities who will be the recipient.

3. Email newsletters to your permission-based list. Use appealing, seasonal content. Include a link back to your website for the full article, and to receive your free gift.

4. Tune up your website. Make sure it's ready for holiday action by setting up specialized landing pages for holiday specials you offer.

5. Get out and network! When people get to know you in person (and they like and trust you), they're far more likely to book your DJ service. So attend business and social gatherings of all kinds.

When conceiving your strategic marketing strategy for getting holiday gigs, remember to include the all-important "full body contact" approach. Kevin Kirouac, owner of City Pro DJ in Edmonton, Alberta, Canada, demonstrates his moves. "Right after an event while happy feelings are running high, I ask a client to rebook us for next year's holiday party. When that's not possible, I contact them on Monday morning with a reminder to book early. Otherwise there's no guarantee our services will be available."

The potential for financial success is in your hands. By being proactive about your efforts, you can achieve holiday sales worth celebrating. Start by placing a festive focus on the gift that keeps on giving – your clients! And many happy returns...

Incorporating Your DJ Service

Maybe you're a part-time mobile operating out of a home office or perhaps you've made it to the "big leagues" and are a multi-system op, conducting business out of a commercial location. In either scenario, does it matter if your company is incorporated? You bet it does, and here's why.

Protection from Personal Liability

Incorporating is one of the best ways to protect yourself as a business owner from personal liability. Shareholders of a corporation are generally not liable for its financial obligations. What's more, creditors may seek payment from the assets of a corporation but not the assets of the shareholders. This means that you can safely engage in your DJ business without fear of risking your home or other personal property.

Conversely, sole proprietors and general partners in a partnership are personally liable for all debts and obligations of the business, such as loans and accounts payable.

The Top 5 Benefits of Incorporating

1. **Limited Liability:** Corporations provide owners and directors protection from personal liability. A corporation exists as a separate structure. Shareholders are not personally liable for corporate debt. If you maintain the corporation's legal status properly and avoid personally guaranteeing the company's obligations, your corporation, and not you, is solely responsible for its own obligations.

2. **Corporate Identity:** "Inc." promotes a business image with credibility, stability, prestige and permanence. Corporations typically want to do business or collaborate with other corporations.

3. **Tax Savings:** Corporations are taxed at a lower rate than individuals, and can offer tax-deductible benefits (e.g., liability, health and life insurance, travel and

entertainment deductions). Tax options are also available by setting up pensions and profit sharing.

4. **Raising Capital:** Investors are more attracted to investing in corporations, and capital is more easily raised through the sale of stock or other equity interests. This may be a more advantageous option than borrowing and making interest payments.

5. **Continuous Life:** Corporations are the most enduring legal entity and do not terminate on the death of the founder, owner or partner, provided it complies with ongoing state and federal paperwork and pays the annual filing fees. Its shares can be transferred. Stock often can be pledged, sold, given away, used as security or given as bonuses.

Forms of Corporations

Here are all of the options to consider:

Limited Liability Company: This hybrid business structure combines the personal asset protection of a "C" Corporation with a partnership's tax flexibility and ease of operation. A properly managed LLC can protect its owners' personal assets from business judgments. Owners can still report their share of company profits or losses on their personal tax returns.

"S" Corporation: This structure refers to a section of the Internal Revenue Code. This election allows business owners to report company profits or losses on their individual tax returns. This business structure also provides owners the opportunity to separate and protect their personal assets from judgments against the business.

"C" Corporation: This structure protects your personal assets from potential judgments against your company; however, the IRS taxes company profits twice, once at the corporate level and again at the shareholder level as dividends. Many business owners consider this "double taxation" a disadvantage.

Sole Proprietorship: This structure is one person alone. He or she will have unlimited liability for all debts of the business, and the income or loss from the business will be reported on his/her personal income tax return along with all other income and expense he or she normally reports.

General Partnership: This structure means that each of the two or more partners will have unlimited liability for the debts of the business. The income and expense is reported on a separate return for tax purposes, but each partner then reports his/her pro-rata share of the profit or loss from the business as one line on his personal tax return.

Limited Partnership: This structure means that each of the general partners has unlimited liability for the debts of the partnership, but the limited partner's exposure to the debts of the partnership is limited to the contribution each has made to the partnership. With certain minor exceptions, the reporting for tax purposes is the same as for a general partnership.

Which One to Choose

In most cases, the best form of corporation for a disc jockey service will be either an LLC (Limited Liability Company) or a Subchapter "S" Corporation. It is also an option to incorporate each division of your company as a separate entity. It is advisable to consult with an attorney to determine exactly what form(s) of organization has the greatest tax and liability advantages for you.

Generating Free Publicity

The value free publicity can generate for your mobile DJ service is enormous. Whether you have just recently opened for business or your company has been around for years, an article (versus an ad) can work wonders. Raising your visibility can help launch a new service or product, and in the end, boost your sales.

What's the key to generating this publicity? Well, as a business owner, you probably have a bit of the self-promoter in you. The trick, it seems, is knowing how to tap into it and, once you've accomplished that, understanding how to alert the media through a properly written press release.

More than just an angle, you need to give the media a genuinely good reason to publish your press release. For example, you can submit one about the opening of your business, a new division, an additional product or service, a staff expansion, location change, or providing sound reinforcement at an upcoming charitable event.

David Gibson, City Editor at the Hartford Courant, is inundated with releases of all kinds. "The most important aspect of a release is to keep it simple," he says. "I usually rewrite a release, and I'm only interested in events that are open to the public. It sometimes helps to include an action-oriented photograph or head-and-shoulder shot."

The first paragraph of your press release should answer these questions: who (is the story about), what (is the story), when (is it occurring), where (is the location) and why (should the editor care). Always list the most important points first, followed by the lesser points. Make sure your message is clear and simple. Proofread the release for spelling and grammatical errors. David suggests, "Send a couple of color action-oriented photographs with your press release. Be sure to identify your company's name, address and phone number along with any photo credits necessary and the names of the people appearing in the photos."

Sample Press Release

FOR IMMEDIATE RELEASE

Project Groove Mobile DJ Company Gives Away Free Dances To Local Schools!

PR Log (Press Release) – Jul 16, 2009 – Due to the current state of the economy, many schools have had to cut their budgets for extracurricular activities such as fun fairs, picnics, proms and dances. In many cases, smaller budgets have led to hiring sub-par entertainment, and some schools have even been forced to cancel their events altogether.

In an effort to help local elementary, middle and high schools with their fiscal dilemma, Project Groove DJs is giving away free dance packages for the 2009-2010 school year through what they call their "Entertainment Stimulus Package" contest.

The idea is the brain-child of Melissa Boger, owner of Project Groove DJs. "No matter what's going on with the economy, people still need to have fun – especially children and teenagers. A dance is a great place for them to release stress and let loose," she says.

Project Groove is a youth-oriented mobile DJ company that provides interactive entertainment packages for the Greater Chicago Area. They also provide disc jockey entertainment for other events, as well. The company is a member of the National Association of Mobile Entertainers (NAME) and is a fully insured.

For more information on Project Groove's "Entertainment Stimulus Package" contest, please visit www.projectgroovedjs.com.

Contact:
Melissa Boger
info@projectgroovedjs.com

#

You can obtain a media list online or at your local library. Send the release to every newspaper, magazine, radio and television station you think may print or air your press release – or better yet, even do a full-blown story on your mobile DJ service. Contact the media to find out their deadlines and the names and titles of the people to whom you should submit your releases. Sending a press release to a specific person versus "City Editor" is extremely important.

"When the media 'talks' about you, it's almost like getting a third-party endorsement," says Mark Ashe, president of Marx Entertainment in Hartford, CT. "Best of all, it doesn't have to cost you a dime!"

Standing Apart from Your Competition

(Co-written with DJ Times writer Jeff Stiles)

The most innovative mobiles possess the ability to creatively "think outside the box" by offering services and products that make them stand apart from their competition. This writer scoured the country to find DJs who dare to be different.

Adam Weitz of A Sharp Production in PA's Huntingdon Valley, has a unique way of getting noticed: he actually sings on the spot to persuade a potential client to hire him for their event. To be prepared, he always carries a karaoke CDG in his briefcase. "When I explain to a client that I sing professionally," he says, "They sometimes ask me to perform for them. I play an upbeat selection and sing with the same energy and theatrics I would use at a party."

Whether at the client's home or at his office, Weitz says that when he performs live for people it usually blows them away, setting him apart from his competition and landing him the event. While his crooning is usually conducted during a private consultation, Weitz says he sometimes will have a potential client visit another client's affair. "I have them page me just as they are arriving so that I can notice when they enter the room," he explains. "As soon as I see them, I start singing a ballad and then go into something festive, upbeat and highly recognizable." Weitz claims this method has been highly effective in booking jobs. Another way Weitz gets clients to notice his talent is to work as a vocal coach with a Bar/Bat Mitzvah celebrant who wants to sing at their party.

Several years ago, DJ Chris James from Mark's Entertainment in Hartford, CT, was trying to find new ways to entertain kids at Bar/Bat Mitzvahs, so he picked up a few books about making balloon animals. He found that this was an easy way to entertain children, make a unique, positive impression on his clients and earn an additional $75 to $125 an hour for this specialty service.

But that's not all James does that's special. While attending a trade show in Las Vegas, he visited a magic shop and learned simple tricks to entertain clients at parties. "I started learning four or five new tricks a week. Now when a client doesn't want music during cocktail hour, sometimes they will go for ballooning and magic, and spend up to $250 for the service."

James finds that such tactics also serve as good audience icebreakers. "I'm getting to know people's first names during this time and letting them know that I'm available to take their song requests later on," he says.

Before getting into a DJ career, James worked as a stand-up comedian in the New York/Boston area. He's appeared on TV's America's Funniest People and has even opened for Adam Sandler. James believes that every good DJ has some natural comedic ability. "We all have to be impromptu when we're performing," he says. "At nearly every event there are golden opportunities to turn common situations into something humorous."

DJ Brian Nicks from Longmeadow, MA, knows how to maximize his opportunities. He once handled sound and lighting at a gig for a comedy basketball team called The Harlem Rockets. The canned music he had been asked to use was choppy, so after the performance, Nicks chatted with the team's manager and offered to produce a custom mix that would enhance the dramatic and comical portions of the show. His offer was accepted, so Nicks created several custom mixes using comical drop-ins, movie themes, popular crowd chants and other sound effects that he felt allowed for show variations that would appeal to different audiences.

The result? The team's manager not only liked Nicks' mixes but was also impressed with his MCing ability and initiative. This proactive DJ was invited to travel with the team to Aruba and Italy to MC their games and handle production. For Brian it all comes down to having vision and being customer-focused. His philosophy: "Do it better every day!"

Veteran MC Randi Rae Treibitz of Major Productions in Edison, NJ, is best known in the DJ community as "The

Mitzvah Maven," the ultimate Bar/Bat Mitzvah party host. However, there is a lesser-known market she also caters to as well: nursing homes and facilities for the handicapped. "I do a one-hour cabaret-style show," she explains. "Some residents are participatory and others are completely comatose. I take people's requests and play lots of music from the '20s, '30s and '40s."

Besides filling in those otherwise idle weekday performance slots, these shows provide Rae with an incredible "feel-good" incentive. "The music brings back memories of happier days for these folks," she says. "I wear bright clothing and a wireless headset so that I can be interactive and walk out among the residents. This allows them to constantly see, be with, and sing along with me."

Rae has to remain emotionally detached to deal with all the sights and smells in nursing homes, and even though the pay isn't great, she believes that by entertaining at long-term care facilities she is improving the quality of life for people who desperately need it – therefore making an important contribution to her community. Rae does get booked for other events by handing out her business cards to the residents' families as well as to doctors, nurses and aides.

Gerry Siracusa, a former "DJ of the Year" contest winner, uses his personality and spontaneity to stand apart from his competition. "I just do whatever comes to me to make the party flow. For me, it's simply a matter of reading a crowd."

Siracusa says he focuses on the client and performs original line dances. "People really don't want to hear the same-old, same-old," he says. "We don't just do 'The Macarena,' 'Electric Slide' and 'The Twist and Shout.' We do have a lot of original ideas that we utilize."

The key to being a professional yet unique DJ, according to this entertainer, is to be educated about clients. "The thing is – and this may seem like a boring answer – it doesn't come down to the line dances or the good-looking entertainer. It comes down to proper business ethics and knowing who your client is, which involves meeting with them and getting to know their interests." In the end, Siracusa says DJs need not be afraid to do something different. "Fear is one of the biggest issues. But don't try to be a non-conformist like everyone else, because a lot of times when you go to DJ shows, they're almost creating cookie-cutter-type nonconformity. So everybody's nonconforming at the same time, making them all conformists."

Sometimes standing out in the crowd simply means taking an existing idea or performance concept to the next level. You don't need to auction off the Best Man's underwear at a wedding reception or dress up in wild costumes to gain attention.

With a little bit of creativity, courage and forethought, we all have the ability to be unique and original with our entertainment offerings. Creating a niche or filling a void in the marketplace is a great place for a savvy DJ to begin.

The Power of Direct Mail Marketing

Many consumers think of direct mail marketing as "junk mail." Business owners often stay away from it because they perceive that this form of marketing has a poor return on investment (ROI). The fact is, if you're not using direct mail as part of your overall marketing campaign, you may be missing a lot more than just an increase in your bottom line.

Most DJs are not marketing gurus and don't know how to design a campaign that's capable of delivering the maximum marketing bang for a minimal marketing buck.

The truth is, the relative cost of direct mail marketing can be high, but if it generates responses that lead to bookings, it is inexpensive marketing and a tax write-off to boot. "Direct mail is always disappointing in the short term," says Brian Doyle of Denon & Doyle in Concord, CA, "But in the long term, it works."

You must know the target market(s) you want to reach and what their "hot buttons" are. For example, wedding lists of couples-to-be can be obtained monthly from your local Wedding Pages directory, which may contain as many as 200 leads. If you want to keep it simple and relatively inexpensive, have 5,000 or 10,000 postcards created, then do your mailing and repeat it one month later.

"The thing about getting these bridal lists is that every DJ Company is doing a mailing," says Doyle. "When you do an additional one a month later, then you're all alone."

It will, of course, be difficult to follow up every one with a phone call, but regardless, you can still expect an average response rate of two to three percent. This is why mass mailing is important. The more people you reach, the higher your response rate will be.

Make 'Em an Offer They Can't Refuse

Ideally, your mailing should entice the prospect to respond to a tantalizing offer so you can sell your service. Appealing to a customer's self-interest is always a key component in your sales message. Which emotional strings can you pull? It helps to know that people are motivated by fun, romance, fear reduction, acceptance, individuality and value.

Of course, you may wish to use a more elaborate package. Your package can consist of an outer envelope, a letter, a brochure or flyer, a response device such as a coupon and a postage-paid return envelope. You may wish to create different direct-mail pieces to target different prospects or markets.

A strong direct-mail piece should contact the following qualities, as are appropriate for your business:

- It creates a sense of urgency and alerts the recipient to the date your offer expires so they know there is a deadline. This will motivate someone to take action rather than think it over.

- It clearly illustrates your unique selling proposition (USP).

- It expresses one clear and powerful idea that focuses on an offer to your prospect. Everything in your mailing should relate to that idea. Reiterate the idea in every piece contained in the mailing.

- It lists your email and website addresses and telephone number(s), and contains a postage-paid reply card for them to send.

- It allows the prospect to pay by major credit card and PayPal.

When designing your materials, it is important to keep in mind that people will initially read the first line of a letter, then the P.S. and the signature, and lastly the entire content of the first paragraph. They will also notice subheads. These parts of the piece must be appealing in order to entice the reader to move on to the rest of the letter, the brochure and the response device.

Many experts feel the response device is the most important item in the package. Be sure it restates your offer briefly but completely. Offer the prospect an irresistible incentive, such as a free basic lighting package or a $50 discount with every booking made by the date that your offer expires. Your goal is to have the prospect financially commit to the booking. This can be accomplished with a deposit of one-third to one-half the total amount, for a booking that can be used any time in the year following the commitment.

Statistics show that the most effective cover letters used for direct mail marketing contain the following elements:

- They are personalized
- They are two-sided and printed in Courier typeface
- They contain headings and subheadings printed in blue
- They are written in conversational language
- The first side ends in the middle of a sentence
- The margins are not justified
- The key points are underlined
- They contain a P.S. at the bottom of the letter
- They use short words, short sentences and short paragraphs
- They use subheads liberally

Mike LoBasso, president of Parameters Entertainment in NY, uses direct mail postcards to increase his wedding business. "My biggest response so far was a mailing I did in January," he says. "I sent out 3,000 pieces the first week of the month. By the end of January, I had 35 responses. I was able to convert many of those into bookings."

It is wise to create or obtain targeted lists for your direct-mail campaign. These lists may include high schools and colleges, banquet facilities, catering halls, engaged couples, Bar/Bat Mitzvahs, corporations, etc. The people and places on your lists should be located within the geographic area your DJ business serves. You may have to do additional research to obtain a specific contact name.

When dealing specifically with schools, you may want to send out separate mailings to the Senior Class Advisor, Student Council President, Student Activities Director, and Junior and Senior Prom Committee.

It is vital that your mailing is sent to and read by the person who has the authority to hire you or to provide a referral to your mobile company. When feasible, follow up the mailing with a telephone call within one week. You may want to call and open the conversation by asking if the information you sent was received and if there are any questions. This person is your contact. Sell them on the virtues of your DJ service.

Don't forget the most important prospects – your past customers. Not only will a satisfied customer likely hire you again but they can also be a goldmine for referrals. Once or twice a year, send direct mailings to contact and companies for whom you have done parties.

Here's an idea you can use as a direct-mail concept: Approach a customer for whom you have entertained at an event, and request their endorsement. Ask them to write a letter on your company's behalf which you will then mail to a prospect list. This letter would be mailed in a stamped envelope with the endorser's return address. Inside would be a simple, one-page letter on the endorser's letterhead. The letter should be straightforward, introduce the writer, and talk about the writer's personal positive experience with your DJ service. Perhaps you can entice this past client by offering a gift certificate for dinner at a nice chain restaurant.

You must carefully measure the effectiveness of your direct-mail campaign to ensure its success. Your success will be measured by the ratio of cost versus return. The three most important things to do if you are to succeed at direct marketing are to test, test, and test.

Larry Neary, a member of the American Marketing Association, says, "Your first piece is called the control piece. If you plan to mail a total of 500 pieces, send 450 to a specific list and 50 with a twist to a similar list. The twist adds or alters something within the piece – a coupon or cassette, for example.

You code both types of pieces to determine which produces a greater response. That becomes the new control piece. This process can be regularly repeated so the response to your direct mail campaign continues to improve."

Test different media, packaging, mailing lists and frequency, Neary urges. Only this testing can give you the certainty needed for commitment.

Over 90% of Americans buy at least one item annually purely as a result of direct marketing. A successful direct-mail campaign that produces significant results is like money in the bank. Your mobile company can cash in on this powerful phenomenon to achieve maximum profits for your business.

Hiring Sub-Contractors vs. Employees

Many multi-ops are confused about the fine points of the law when it comes to whether they have employees or independent contractors working for or with them. The difference is huge and it's important to determine the correct legal status, or it could cost you a bundle.

As an employer, you must keep separate payroll records for each employee; withhold federal income, Social Security and Medicare taxes; withhold state income and other state taxes; prepare quarterly and year-end payroll tax returns; pay the employer's portion of Social Security, Medicare and unemployment taxes; purchase Workers Compensation Insurance; and prepare year-end earnings statements for each employee.

If this sounds like quite the ... ahem ... taxing endeavor, that's because it is. Some small business organizations estimate that all this can cost you an additional 30% of your payroll.

One way of avoiding such a burdensome expense is to hire independent contractors. But just what is a sub- or independent contractor? According to the IRS, people in business for themselves are not considered employees. Also, independent contractors usually have business cards, a business bank account and printed invoice forms.

If you do utilize independent contractors, it's important that they understand that you are not paying them as an employee, which means you are not responsible for taxes, insurance or Social Security. An independent contractor is not eligible for unemployment insurance. Many mobile companies get into costly trouble with federal and state governments when former sub-contractors complain to the IRS after being turned down for unemployment insurance or fined for not paying their own Social Security.

Who Is An Employee?

Let's say you've decided to go the employee route. Be aware that the IRS is more likely to consider a person as an employee and not an independent contractor if they: use your tools, materials and equipment instead of their own; receive on-the-job training; follow hours that you set; work specifically according to your instructions; hire or supervise your workers; and receive health insurance, sick pay, vacation pay or similar employee benefits.

To establish an employee-employer relationship, more emphasis will generally be placed upon the employer's right to exercise direction and control (regardless of whether such right is actually exercised), the right to hire and fire, the relationship of the work to the employer's business, and the degree of work performed (continuous, intermittent, etc).

Let's say in your mind, you have established an employer-employee relationship. You now go to your insurance carrier who will handle workers' compensation. These following questions are designed by the carriers to determine how much control exists. The more control you have over the employee, the more likely that they will be regarded as such. These questions vary from state to state, and are decided by the subjective opinion of the carrier. Remember, if an incorrect determination is made, the insurance carrier can be liable, so rest assured the process will be a stringent one.

1. What is the type of work performed by the contractor?

2. Does contractor have his/her own workers' comp coverage?

3. Is there a written contract between company and contractor?

4. Does the company have the right to terminate the contract without prior notice?

5. Does the company have the right to hire and fire the contractor or his/her assistants?

6. Does the contractor have the right to work for others? If yes, does he/she do so?

7. Does the employer withhold social security, unemployment, state or federal taxes from amounts paid to the contractor?

8. Is the contractor permitted to choose his/her own work hours?

9. Does the contractor have the right to reject assignments?

10. Does the contractor furnish his/her own tools and equipment?

11. Does the contractor furnish all or a portion of materials?

12. Does the contractor have his/her own place of business?

13. Does the contractor advertise such business in the Yellow Pages?

14. Is the contractor paid on a distinctly different basis than regular employees?

15. Does the contractor have the right to terminate the contract without penalty?

16. State methods of payment: flat amount, hourly, daily, or weekly amount.

Tom McCloskey, a New Jersey-based attorney for entertainment companies, states, "There is no definitive answer to the employee vs. independent contractor question because laws vary from state to state."

There are advantages and disadvantages to having employees and independent contractors. Independent contractors, for example, are responsible for paying their own taxes. Employees have taxes deducted from their paychecks. To avoid a potential theft or lawsuit nightmare, independent contractors should provide property and liability insurance on their equipment, unless the mobile company they work for provides it. It is a good idea for mobile companies with equipment and employees to cover both under their insurance policy. If there is ever a claim (lawsuit) from a client, it will be made against the company they have contracted with, not an individual DJ.

There are also tax benefits to hiring DJ employees if you have numerous people working for you and multiple locations. If you hire employees and provide benefits, it may make your company more attractive to the talent in your market. You also may be able to pay employees less than independents.

Of course, the best advantage to hiring employees, as opposed to independent contractors, is the ability to give your multi-system company a degree of uniformity. Since you legally don't train independent contractors, product consistency, over the long term, may be a problem if you make it your policy to hire this way.

It's important to clarify key issues in a formal, written contract between your company and its DJ employees and/or subcontractors. One such issue is exclusivity. According to McCloskey, "Mobile DJs who work exclusively for one company can still be considered independent contractors. The use of a restrictive covenant in a contract restricts a DJ from competing with the company they are currently working for. It usually contains a specific geographic area and time frame in which the DJ can not compete. A contract with a sub or employee should clearly state how and the manner in which payment is made."

The IRS looks at the manner in which compensation is given. DJs who sign a full-time or part-time employment agreement are considered by the IRS to be employees. An employee may receive a flat weekly salary and medical benefits or an hourly wage for work performed.

Employees often receive an employment manual at the start of a new job. Such a manual generally provides details on the company, its operations and its policies, and its procedures. A mobile service can provide a similar manual to its independent contractor DJs. However, it must contain conspicuous boldfaced disclaimers that it is not to be construed as a contract of employment. The fact that the company imposes requirements on its DJs is not to be construed as an employer/employee relationship. It is strongly advised that you have a lawyer write this manual for your business.

Sara Lavery is a mobile DJ from Bristol, CT, has worked as both an employee and a subcontractor, and wouldn't want it any other way. "I like having jobs handed to me on a silver platter," she says. "I don't have to worry about the expense of buying equipment, or advertising or overhead. I may not make as much money as someone who owns their own company, but I don't have the heartaches, either."

Whichever road you decide to travel, be sure to make an informed decision. Get advice from an attorney regarding the employment laws in your state. Have proper contracts and manuals written by an expert. The expense incurred on the front end can be far less than the cost of fighting the IRS or going into litigation later on.

Is Your DJ Service a One-Hit Wonder?

If your company offers "Professional Mobile DJ Services for All Occasions," you may be reeling from an increase in local competition due to the vast number of newbies entering the mix over the past several years.

With competitors popping up around every corner and your profit margin spiraling downward, diversification of your company's offerings could amplify your stronghold in the marketplace.

There is an upsurge of disc jockey companies that also offer full production services, amusements, trivia, lighting effects, casino tables, digital photos, party props, dancers/party motivators, video and photography.

Dare to Be Different

Lisa Kasberg, owner of I'm a Girl DJ Entertainment in Los Angeles, CA offers the latter service with a twist; Photo Guest Books at weddings and Photo Memory Books at Bar/Bat Mitzvahs. "Our photographer takes digital pictures of the guests during an event. They are printed on the spot, and then placed into an elegant book where, next to their photo, people can write special words to the guest(s) of honor. The book is given to the celebrant(s) as a memento."

Adding this product to her repertoire nets Kasberg an extra $400-600 per event. She does the upsell by showing a sample book during her initial client presentation.

What dynamic range of offerings should you cue up? It's best to capitalize on your existing areas of expertise, expand your know-how through investigation and education, or form "power partnerships" with other companies that have synergistic services or products that are out of your reach, and share the profits.

New Jersey's Lou Polino of Dynamic Crew has made his business omni-directional by becoming a "one-stop shop" for his clientele. His varied ventures keep funds rolling in from several avenues. "In addition to the standard DJ services, we are based inside of a tuxedo shop, and offer limousines, photography and video. People really like the convenience of being able to get just about everything they need for their event right here."

Carpe Diem

In 1977 when one DJ decided to call himself "Professor Jam," little did he know that one day he would expand his groove to become Founding Director of the Computer DJ Summit/Convention in Atlanta, GA, now in its sixth year of operation.

Being resourceful and thinking outside the box has increased his non-DJ revenue by nearly 25%; however, the diversification spirit came to Jam with humble beginnings. "I began by augmenting my DJ services with party props, then theme decorations. For many years I had limited success with these products. Later, I included high-quality printing for my school, wedding, and corporate clients. This produced much better results."

Jam also seizes unexpected opportunities by going the extra mile. Here's an example. "Recently at a bridal show, a couple asked if I could obtain an unusual item for their wedding – an old fashioned photo booth that prints a strip of pics. I did some research, found what they wanted, and am in the contract phase of obtaining one right now. I'm confident this new product will be a big hit with my clients."

To gain buy-in, Jam uses a soft-sell approach with prospects by simply showing them all of his services online. He reassures them that whether or not they hire him as a DJ, his other offerings are still available. This approach has worked well because over the years he has received checks for non-DJ items when he had only brief initial contact with someone and was never contracted as "the entertainer."

Roll with the Changes

Marx Entertainment in Hartford, CT, received press and notoriety when they provided entertainment for the President of the United States. In business for a quarter of a century, owner Mark Ashe has learned a lot about the value of good public relations and branching out. "Over the years we have continually expanded our number of DJs and systems, as well as our in-house services. We started with just mobile entertainment and then kept spreading out – always keeping our services in-house. Over the years my company has added dancers, videography, virtual reality and sports games, casino tables, photo booths, and the list keeps growing."

To keep pace with the changes in his business, Mark changed the name of his company from Mark's Rolling Dance Revue to Marx Entertainment. He won't say exactly how much his profits have increased as a result of broadening his horizons, but Ashe laughs and tells this writer it's "a lot."

Having an entrepreneurial instinct and a nose for business goes a long way toward knowing when to strike while the iron is hot. Orlando, FL-based J.R. Silva sets a positive example. "I have developed two new services and a new company to my existing lineup: Text Live (Text to Screen production) and Silva Video, which includes PowerPoint and Photoshop graphics. We do everything in-house. As needed, I hire folks from nearby art schools and colleges who have the skills to work these various programs."

Silva discovered Text Live while at a trade show four years ago. He performed research and felt it was well suited for the types of video events he was performing. He made an agreement with the company to exclusively represent the product, and is now a dealer for them. "I upsell our new services by showing our standard production and then our enhanced production. It's a compare-and-contrast sales method, and people are able to see a big difference. I am careful to spend the time making sure a client really wants and can afford our bigger offering."

Silva says that with the addition of his new services, his profit margins are "very good." He runs both companies out of one office, sharing personnel across two entertainment companies.

Increase Your Gain with Input

Diversification can help your company weather tough times by providing alternate sources of revenue. Before making an overture, remember to ask for input from clients, colleagues, friends, family, and respected business folk with whom you network. Their feedback will let you know if you're properly grounded, or in need of some further monitoring before phasing in something new.

Lou Polino offers some advice on what to expect if you provide multiple services. "It's difficult to spend time, energy, and money in several areas rather than being able to focus on just one. I have to really stay on top of things to make sure that nothing in my operation suffers from lack of attention."

If your DJ business is a one-hit wonder, you can master the comeback with a remix of your service offerings by finding a strategic sweet spot that is in tune with you, your business, and your marketplace.

With encores coming your way, soon you might even be ready for a megamix.

Commanding the Crowd

"Ladies and gentlemen, may I please have your attention? Ahem. Folks, may I have your attention up here please. **I HAVE AN IMPORTANT ANNOUNCEMENT TO MAKE, SO KINDLY DIRECT YOUR ATTENTION TO THE DJ NOW!**"

Have you ever found yourself in a situation where seemingly uninterested or downright rude guests at an event would not quiet down long enough to allow you to make an announcement on the mic?

Many DJs experience this dilemma but don't know what to do differently to truly command an audience. Surely there must be some "tricks of the trade" to help a frustrated emcee, right? There are, and DJ Times found them from some "master mobiles on the mic" around the country.

What do you first say on the mic to grab the crowd's attention?

Matt Peterson of Peterson Productions in Northampton, MA, estimates that the average audience does not listen to the first seven to ten words that are spoken on the microphone. "I lower the volume of the music, wait a few seconds and then welcome everyone to the event. I acknowledge the venue then the guest(s) of honor and lastly my staff and myself."

Hartford, CT-based Mark Ashe of Marx Entertainment turns off the music altogether. "Many DJs make the mistake of trying to talk over the music and make themselves sound more like an announcer over a PA system rather than an entertainer commanding attention. Talking with a crowd rather than talking to the crowd will have a much more engaging affect with you audience."

J.R. Silva of Orlando's Silva Entertainment uses a more personalized and informal approach. "Usually, to get people's attention, I will use the guest of honor's name in some manner. 'Hey friends, Gina and Bob have asked me to get everyone's attention.' On other occasions, I may do a sound check on mic, such as, 'Good evening friends and family, can everyone hear me okay? We have a lot to celebrate and we want everyone to be in on the fun, so I want to make sure now that we have everyone's attention and that our friends in back are able to hear me, too. If you can hear me well in the back areas of the ballroom raise your hand in the air.'"

What music programming techniques do you use to fill a dance floor and build the energy there?

Popular Arizona jock DJ Soulman believes that it's better to be proactive than reactive when it comes to filling a dance floor because once people sit down, you may not get a second chance to get them up again. "To lure people out, I always use what I call 'party bait.' This could be a classic hit or last month's hot track. Then I play hit after hit to keep them dancing. There are always plenty of tracks to play that will keep the crowd jumping and having fun. Sometimes I will say, 'Okay, we need all the ladies on the dance floor. Ladies only, no guys.' Then I'll play something current and popular with women. Other times I'll get the crowd going with an interactive dance."

Elite Entertainment's Mike Walter of NJ plays sure-fire hits and gets on the mic to invite people to join in the festivities. "My tone and mannerisms are in many ways even more important than the words I choose. I smile, use eye contact and big gestures so that everyone in the room can see me. These things are important and they convey the message I am trying to deliver."

Also from NJ, Steve Cie uses group dances as his primary tool. Depending on the age of the audience, a slow dance or a high energy club dance tune is also in his arsenal. Silva uses the celebrant's names to promote dancing. "I say, 'Bob and Jennifer would like to invite all the couples present to join them on the dance floor.' Other times, I point out that we need at least one couple from each party table to join them. It can snowball from there and turn into a classic multiplication dance. I also have dances from different decades that I can lead as an ice breaker to get the dance floor moving."

What do you do when there are unruly youngsters at an event who are being noisy and taking away the spotlight from the celebrant(s)?

Ashe recognizes the importance of handling the situation with "kid gloves." "If it's a Mitzvah, and it usually is, our dancers are really good at pulling a kid to the side and changing his/her attitude. This is a delicate situation because even though someone might be a distraction to the party, he/she also might be a future client."

Silva tries to ignore them at first; then if things get too out of hand, he meets with the kids offstage and off mic. "I talk with them so they'll be aware that I feel they are being rude or distracting. I even say things like, 'How did you get on the Guest List? It doesn't seem like you're aware of why we're all here tonight.' At times I have had to threaten the youngsters that I will contact the event sponsors and have them asked to leave. But that rarely happens once they understand how much I care for the event and my client."

What do you do when someone asks for your microphone to make an announcement at an event?

Every mobile we spoke to said that they do not give their microphone away to anyone. To ensure that he doesn't have to, 35-year industry veteran Cie takes it one step further. "It stipulates in my contract that all announcements are to be made by me. I screen all requests to determine if they are appropriate and if not, I nicely let the person know that I cannot make that particular announcement."

DJ Adam Tiegs from Milton, WA, handles the request gingerly. "I let the person know that I will gladly make the announcement and ask what they want said. Depending on what a client indicates to us beforehand regarding how active they'd like me to be on the mic, I may or may not move forward with the announcement."

What do you do to take charge of the situation when a fight breaks out at an event?

An open bar combined with a party can sometimes be a recipe for a drunken brawl. At the very least, when guests consume too much liquor they can become demanding and belligerent, so what's a DJ to do? According to Walter, this is an occupational hazard, but there is a way to deal with it. "I'd say the rule of thumb is to try to defuse the situation with a confrontation that is kind, short and sweet. I don't try to explain myself to drunk guests. For example, if someone is insisting on a song that the bride and groom don't want played, then they can ask and re-ask for it but it's not going to happen. I just smile and say, 'Let me see if I can get to that one,' and then just hope the guy forgets about it. If there's a fight, I wait until it's resolved before refocusing the guests on the fact that they're at a celebration."

Peterson recommends turning off the music immediately if a fight breaks out and remaining calm. "Don't get involved in any drunken disputes. Act professionally, CYA and protect yourself, your staff and your equipment. Be sure to have a security clause in your entertainment agreement that supports you this situation. Choose your venues and clients carefully."

How do you help a wedding couple achieve the "WOW" factor at their reception?

Tieg tries to get a feel of who they are and what they want. "I try to determine how much attention a couple wants me to give them over the mic. I also suggest additional entertainment options for cocktail hour such as having a magician. For clients who want a lot of guest interaction at their reception, I recommend activities like the Kissing Game and Anniversary Countdown Dance. Keeping guests thoroughly entertained is the key to making an event memorable."

DJ Soulman gives examples of what he has done in the past that works well and gives options to couples. "I also remind them that we do several weddings a month and they are only having one, so it's our job to give ideas and suggestions. By working together, we can plan the best reception possible."

Las Vegas-based club jock AL3 is the official DJ of the UFC and National DJ Champion. He commands a crowd on the dance floor based on demographics and if a promoter or General Manager hires him for a specific sound or theme for the night. No matter what, though, he infuses his own personality and soul into the music he mixes and plays. "I start the opening vibe by playing a set of familiar music at a good tempo to motivate the crowd to dance. If you're a good DJ in a decent club the dance floor will become filled when people are ready."

As professional entertainers, we have all dealt with less-than-ideal circumstances under which we needed to "step up" and command the crowd; however, Peterson reminds us to think of each party we do as a blessing. "As the chosen entertainer, YOU are now responsible for the event. So, be sure your equipment and music library are up to date, your staff is well-informed and you are well-prepared. Always be respectful of your client's wishes and be willing to lend a helping hand if need be at the special occasion."

WEDDING ENTERTAINMENT AGREEMENT

This agreement, dated <<ContSent>> between XYZ Entertainment, hereinafter referred to as "Company", and «Ms» «ClientFirst» «ClientLast» and/or «Mr» «GroomFirst» «GroomLast» herein referred to as "Client" are both jointly and separately responsible for total contract execution. In consideration of the mutual covenants herein contained, and other good and valuable consideration, the Company and the Client hereto agree as follows:

1. Company agrees to provide a Disc Jockey herein referred to as "DJ" on «Date», a «Day», for a event at «Loc», «LocAdd1», «LocCity», «LocST», «LocZIP» to begin at «Time» for up to «Hours» hours, which must conclude on or before «DoneBy». Company also agrees to provide Client with an Entertainment Coordinator to assist in the planning of the event.

2. Client agrees to pay Company a total fee of «Tot», to be paid to in two or more payments.

3. A contract signing payment of $300.00 in US currency in cash, valid check, money order or major credit card including VISA, MasterCard, American Express or Discover, and the signed contract, must be in Company's possession on or before «ContDue». This payment is non refundable. Please make all checks payable to "XYZ Entertainment."

4. If this Contract is not signed and returned, and the initial payment is not made on or before the contract signing due date, Company will not guarantee the availability of a DJ for event.

5. Company must receive the balance of payments totaling «Bal» by any of the payment methods noted above in Item #3 of this contract on or before «PayBy». A fee of $35.00 is to be paid for returned bank checks.

6. Payments are not transferable, not assignable, nor refundable except as explicitly described in this contract.

7. Client' satisfaction is guaranteed or the Client may request a partial or full refund of the final payment. The guarantee covers those actions and decisions that are under the Company's and/or DJ's direct control and supervision only. Client agrees to notify the Company of any dissatisfaction immediately. This guarantee expires seventy-two hours after the conclusion of the event.

8. Should Client desire additional time beyond the contracted «Hours» hours then DJ, Client, and facility must unanimously agree to extra time extensions. Client agrees to pay DJ by valid check payable to "XYZ Entertainment" in the amount of $150.00 for each half hour of extra time. Client further agree that extended time payments must be paid to the prior to beginning the extended time period.

9. Client agree to complete "Event Planner" and "Song List" available to them online at Company's website, http://www.xyzent.com, no less than two weeks prior to «Date».

10. (a) Client and/or their agents are to ensure and to provide DJ with unencumbered, and non hazardous access into, and through the loading area, facility, and work space, at least 1 ½ hour prior to guests arrival at event and then immediately upon conclusion of event; one 115 volt 20 amp duplex grounded electrical outlet, free of other connected electrical devices located/positioned within 10 feet of DJ's setup; an approx. 6-foot banquet-style table preferably centered in front of the dance floor in an area that provides ample space for DJ's equipment including speakers (and lighting stand, truss, and/or screens if applicable). All Client/Agent provided extension cords must be 3-conductor 14-gauge wire, not to exceed 25 feet in length, and be safely secured and installed in advance of Company's arrival.
(b) If the event is being held outdoors, the client is to additionally provide overhead shelter with protection from sun and rain for DJ, DJ's equipment and

recordings. The size of overhead shelter will be no less than 8' x 8' in diameter. If an approx. 6-foot banquet style table will not be provided, Client must notify DJ at least 48 hours prior to «Date».
(c) Company agrees that DJ will keep the set-up area under his/her direct control safe and will maintain a general liability insurance policy.

11. Company and DJ will retain exclusive rights over the event production and presentation, including but not limited to, the details, means, and methods of services except as agreed upon by the Company's and Client. Should the Client or their agents exercise partial or full control of Company's music selections, equipment setup location, content, programming, timing, and/or system volume, the Company is indemnified and released from all implied or specific guarantees.

12. A Company representative and/or DJ may take photographs and/or videotape at event. Client gives Company the right to print, publish, and use these freely for marketing purposes. (Client: If permission is not granted, initial here_____)

13. DJ's performance is for the personal enjoyment of Client. Unauthorized commercial use of any photographs, videos, and/or recordings of the DJ's performance without the expressed written consent of the Company is prohibited.

14. Client and/or their agents agrees that they hold all necessary authorizations, fees, licenses and/or permits as may be required or mandated by the facility, local, state, and/or federal codes or law.

15. Client is responsible and liable for the results and costs of, any/all injury or damage by them, their guests and/or agents, to the DJ's person, equipment, vehicles, and peripherals. Connection of Client, guest, vendor, or facility provided internal or external input or output devices into or out of the DJ's equipment is strictly prohibited.

16. Should DJ become seriously ill or injured, suffer catastrophic equipment loss, death of a loved one or other extraordinary unforeseen acts of God, nature and/or fate, the Company agrees to take prudent action, circumstances permitting, to provide the Client with an alternative DJ, services, or a full refund of all payments.

17. If Client has to terminate Company's services, the Client agree to the following conditions: (1) less than 60-days prior to «Date», no refund will be issued, (2) more than 60 but less than 90-days prior to «Date», only the initial contract signing payment of $300.00 will be refunded, (3) more than 90 but less than 120-days prior to «Date», 50% of the total fee «Tot» will be refunded, (4) more than 120-days prior to «Date», the total fee «Tot» minus the initial signing payment of $300.00 will be refunded.

18. If Client has to terminate Company's services due to extreme inclement weather on «Date», Company must be given a minimum of 24 hours advance notice and concur with the termination. In this circumstance, Company will apply a total fee of «Tot» toward a future event date if Company and Client sign a new contract within thirty days of Client terminating Company's services. Any new date requested by Client is subject to DJ's availability.

19. The maximum contract liability of the Company or Client will be no greater than «Tot» as specified in Item #2 of this contract. If any portion of this contract is held to be invalid, it will not invalidate the validity or enforceability of all remaining contract provisions.

20. The Client agrees that any and all modifications to any portion of this contract by the Client must be submitted in writing, be approved in writing, and must be signed by the Company or the modifications are invalid and nonbinding.

21. Client agrees to indemnify and hold Company and DJ harmless from any and all claims, liabilities, damages and expenses arising from the actions of Client, its agents, representatives, contractors and guests whether invited

or uninvited. Should any contractual dispute not be mutually resolved, Company and Client agree to litigate the matter subject to the laws of the State of New Jersey, which govern this contract. The Client agrees that the venue for settling a dispute will be in a court located in Camden County, New Jersey. The losing party agrees to pay all court and legal fees associated with the enforcement of this contract. The Client and Company will indemnify, defend, and hold the other harmless from any and all other claims, demands, losses, suits, proceedings, penalties, expenses, or other liabilities, including attorney fees and court costs, arising out of or resulting from the performance of this agreement except as contained herein.

22. This contract contains all the agreements by the parties hereto. There are no promises, agreements, terms, or conditions other than those contained herein. This agreement will apply to and bind all parties, and may not be assigned or transferred by either party.

AGREED TO AND ACCEPTED BY:

Signature:

X_____

____

«Ms» «ClientFirst» «ClientLast» (Client)

Dated: X_____

Signature:

X_____

____

Dated: X_____

«Mr» «GroomFirst» «GroomLast» (Client)

Signature:

_____

___

Dated: _____

John Doe, Owner, on behalf of XYZ Entertainment

Appendix

Author-Recommended Mobile DJ Industry Resources

BOOKS

- *Making Money as a Mobile Entertainer* by Raymond A. Mardo III (Amazon.com)

- *Mind Your Business* by Larry Williams (PlanetDJ.com)

- *Music from My Heart and Performance Beyond Expectation* by Ray Martinez (DJraymar@aol.com

- *Spinnin' 2000* by Bob Lindquist & Dennis Hampson (Amazon.com)

- *The Best Wedding Reception Ever* by Peter Merry (Amazon.com)

- *The Complete Disc Jockey* by Stu Chisholm (MobileBeat.com)

- *The Master Wedding MC* by Ken Day (MobileBeat.com)

- *The Mobile DJ Handbook* and *The DJ Sales & Marketing Handbook* by Stacy Zemon (For a personally autographed copy, visit ProMobileDJ.com)

- *The Ultimate Book of DJ Games* by Sid Vanderpool (DJzone.com/store)

CHAT SITES

- DJchat.com

- OurDJtalk.com

- Start.MobileBeat.com

- WorldWideDJs.org

CLIENT TIPS

- Weekly Wedding Tips (Weekly-Wedding-Tips.com)
- Weekly Bar/Bat Mitzvah Tips (Bar-Bat-Mitzvah-Tips.com)

CONSULTANTS

Business, Sales, Marketing & Copywriting

- Stacy Zemon (StacyZemon.com)

MC Training for DJ Companies

- Johnny K (DJtrainingSite.com)

Performance Enhancement Techniques

- Paul "The DJ Coach" Kida (TheDJCoach.com/DJcoach@mobilebeat.com)

Website Design, Rewriting, Copy Editing, Proofreading & Styling

- Bryan "The Grammar Hawk" Durio (DrProof.com)

Website Marketing

- Adam Scott (ascot21@gmail.com)

CONVENTIONS, SHOWS, CONFERENCES & CRUISES

- Appalachian Regional Mobile DJ Symposium (ArmDJs.com)
- BPM (VisitBPM.co.uk)
- Canadian DJ Show (CDJshow.com)
- DJ Cruise (DJcruise.com)
- International DJ Expo (DJtimes.com)
- Mobile Beat DJ Show & Conference (MobileBeat.com)

- Musikmesse (musik.messefrankfurt.com/frankfurt/en/besucher/willkommen.html)
- National Association of Music Merchants (Namm.com)
- WeDJ Cruise (WeDJcruise.com)

DVDs

- Bobby Morganstein Productions DVD Series & Party CD Series (BMPcd.com)
- The 1% Solution Series by Randy Bartlett (DJOnePercentSolution.com)
- The Game Master Series by Scott Faver (MobileBeat.com)
- The Interactive Party Host by Johnny K (DJtrainingSite.com)
- Training Your Next Great DJ by Mike Walter (TrainingYourNextGreatDJ.com)

EDUCATIONAL WEBSITES

- DiscJockey101.com
- DJU.MobileBeat.com
- DJzone.com
- Raymardo.com
- The DJ Rebirth (TheDJRebirth.com)

MAGAZINES/NEWS SOURCES

- Disc Jockey News Network (DJNN.com)
- DJ Times magazine (Djtimes.com)
- Mobile Beat magazine (MobileBeat.com)
- Pro Mobile magazine (ProMobile.org.uk)

MUSIC & VIDEO

- Promo Only Music & Video (PromoOnly.com)

SCHOOLS/TRAINING

- Computer DJ Summit (ComputerDJsummit.com)
- DJ Training Center & Studio (DJtrainingcenter.com)
- Florida Academy of Mobile Entertainment (FameDJschool.com)

SOFTWARE

- DJ Intelligence (IntelligenceInc.com)
- DJ Webmin (DJwebmin.com)

SOUND & LIGHTING EQUIPMENT

- American DJ Lighting (AmericanDJ.com)
- Cortex Digital Music Controller (Cortex-Pro.com)
- Denon DJ (DenonDJ.com)
- Neutral Buoyancy Speaker Stands (Frankenstand.com)

UNIQUENESS ARSENAL

- Audible Memories 2.0 (Audible-Memories.com)
- Dollar Dance Plus (OutsideTheBox.biz/Dollar-Dance-Plus/c22/index.html)
- Text Live (TextLive.com)

NOTE: The author is not responsible for the products or services of the individuals, businesses, organizations or manufacturers listed in this Appendix. Apologies are made for any accidental errors or omissions.

Train Your DJs Right...

From the Start!

Do you believe it's possible to find talent and teach them how to DJ your way? If so, then this is the one product you'll need!

This two-disc set contains a training DVD and a CD-ROM with all of the documents required to monitor your trainees progress.

The DVD contains 16 complete hands-on training sessions and the CD-ROM contains Contracts, Quizzes, a Power Point Music History Lesson, a Final Test and a Diploma.

BIO: Mike Walter has been spreading the gospel of recruitment and training for over a decade. He has been a featured speaker at DJ conventions and a writer for trade publications. Mike is also the Producer of the International DJ Expo "DJ of the Year" competition held annually in Atlantic City. He is the owner of Elite Entertainment, a successful NJ-based multi-system operation that has been selected by Modern Bride magazine and The Knot as a top entertainment company in the country.

> *"There are few people in our industry as qualified as Mike Walter to teach DJ business owners how to train their entertainment staff. This DVD and CD-ROM set takes all the guess work out of the learning process and thoroughly covers every area of importance. It's a "no-brainer" that better talent equals more bookings and a bigger bottom-line for your company."* - **Stacy Zemon**

Training Your Next Great DJ is Just $250 (S&H Included) at TrainingYourNextGreatDJ.com

Mike Walter is available to Multi-Op business owners for one-on-one mentoring sessions.

Contact him to discuss your company's needs at Mchl88@aol.com.

iKEY-AUDIO

www.iKEY-AUDIO.com

M^{V2} Series

M10S^{V2}

M-606^{V2}

M10S^{V2}   M-808^{V2}   M-606^{V2}   M-505^{V2}

GCI Technologies
1 Mayfield Avenue
Edison, NJ USA   08837-3820
Tel : 1-732-346-0061· Fax : 1-732-346-0065
Email : sales@gci-technologies.com

Turbo-Charge Your DJ Career!

with these best-selling books from author Stacy Zemon

Available at ProMobileDJ.com

The Mobile DJ Handbook

How to Start & Run a Profitable Mobile Disc Jockey Service

This is the world's best-selling disc jockey book, which has helped many thousands of mobiles to build their businesses and incomes. It covers the nuts-and-bolts issues you need to know to successfully start and run your mobile entertainment company and earn top dollar.

Topics Covered Include: Performance and Professionalism; Equipment and Music; Sales and Marketing; Clients; Employees; Interactive Dances; Booking Opportunities; Tips from Successful DJ Business Owners, Sample Contracts, Forms and Marketing Materials, and lots more.

The DJ Sales & Marketing Handbook

How to Achieve Success, Grow Your Business and Get Paid to Party!

This book provides a road map for securing more events and becoming the highest paid DJ in your market. It is an essential reference manual jam-packed with practical tools, expert tips and cost-effective methods for achieving dramatic results.

Topics Covered Include How to: Create and Implement a Marketing Plan; Convert Prospects into Loyal Clients; Generate Free Publicity; Make Important Strategic Alliances; Maximize Your Profits and much, much more.